WHAT

MW01141687

COURAGE TO FIND THE FIRE WITHIN

"Peter Hobler has a passion for empowering people to move past their subconscious fears to realize their fullest potential, and a gift for bringing out their very best from within through his practical teachings. His remarkable talent has been refined from years of 'walking the walk' and teaching from real-world experience. Let Peter's gift of wisdom both inspire and transform you!"

– JT DeBolt, Mission Accomplishment Expert

"Peter's inspiration, insights and guidance have led me to understand how my subconscious fears had been holding me back. I have learned how to look at my short-term and long-term goals and for the first time in my life have developed a plan of action. I am applying the principles Peter is teaching into my life and I am developing a more self-empowering mindset. I am learning how to actually make progress toward my goals."

– Tim Dodson

"Peter, thank you for inspiring me to find the courage to confront change and enable me to develop in both my personal and business lives. Your upfront and calm guidance has helped me look beyond my previously self-prescribed limits and to see the potential I have to offer.

I am amazed at how much more I accomplish when applying your methods and following your suggestions. My goals and dreams are now that much closer since you and I have been working together."

– Daryl Watterson

Get clarity for your destination, Discover your passion, prepare your courage and live life with purpose, passion, inspiration and gratitude.

Peter Hobler

COURAGE

TO FIND THE

FIRE

WITHIN

INVEST IN YOURSELF
TO DISCOVER YOUR
PASSION

PETER HOBLER

ALOHA
PUBLISHING

COURAGE TO FIND THE FIRE WITHIN
INVEST IN YOURSELF TO DISCOVER YOUR PASSION
By Peter Hobler

Copyright © 2013
Aloha Publishing
Boise, Idaho
www.alohapublishing.com

Edited by Kim Foster
Cover Design by Cari Campbell, Cari Campbell Design
Interior Design by Shiloh Schroeder, Fusion Creative Works

ISBN: 978-1-61206-054-5

Second Printing, 2013

Published in the United States of America

LIVE, LEARN, LOVE

by Alie Hobler

Every day

I look outside my window

And I see the same thing.

Every day

I look inside me

And I see something different.

DEDICATION

In Memory...

of my younger brother and best friend, Chris Hobler, who lost his battle with Amyotrophic Lateral Sclerosis on February 16, 2005. Chris, know your efforts and your passion to find cures and improve the lifestyle of individuals with neurological diseases via the public charity Hope Happens for Neurological Disorders and the collaborative research laboratory The Hope Center for Neurological Disorders was and still is truly inspirational. Your memory via your inspiration will live on forever as it impacts the lives of many.

Dedicated with true gratitude, to the three most special women in my life:

To my Mom, Jean Hobler, for always being there no matter what.

To my daughter, Alie. May the contents of this book inspire you to recognize the truly amazing and beautiful potential inside of you.

Kathy, thank you for your limitless love and support which you have consistently demonstrated in so many ways during the past eight years.

Also…

To everyone young or old, no matter what your background or life's experiences, who has the tenacity to discover your passion and the desire to make the commitment to wake up and look within to recognize your potential…and the courage to take action to realize your potential.

This includes Jeremy Savannah and all of the other mentees in the Join Hands Mentoring Program in East St. Louis. It's with this gratitude that 10 percent of the net income from this book will be donated to Join Hands to support you, with the intent to teach and inspire you to recognize your potential and find your passion so you can live life the way you really deserve.

CONTENTS

Introduction: Know Your Passion 11

Preface: Who I Am and Why I Can Help 13

Chapter 1: **How I Found My Passion** 19

Chapter 2: **The FIRE Within You** 31

Chapter 3: **The Elements of FIRE** 35

Chapter 4: **The 7 Principles of COURAGE** 43

Chapter 5: **COURAGE Principle 1**: Clarity of Destination 49

Chapter 6: **COURAGE Principle 2**: Origin of Inspiration 53

Chapter 7: **COURAGE Principle 3**: Unrealized Potential 63
= Mind-set

Chapter 8: **COURAGE Principle 3**: Unrealized Potential Cont. 73
Forging Your New Mind-set: Forming New Habits,
Routines, and Rituals

Chapter 9: **COURAGE Principle 4**: Responsibility 91

Chapter 10: **COURAGE Principle 5**: Awareness of What 97
Is Holding You Back and Stopping the Vicious
Cycle of Subconscious Fear

Chapter 11: **COURAGE Principle 6**: Gratitude 109

Chapter 12: **COURAGE Principle 7**: Excellence 119

Chapter 13: **Consistency and Patience: Foundations** 127
for Success

Chapter 14: **What Will It Take for You?** 131

Acknowledgements 137

About the Author 141

INTRODUCTION

KNOW YOUR PASSION

Sharing, teaching, coaching, and inspiring people to prepare the courage to find the fire within is truly my passion. My goal is to help committed individuals discover their inspiration and passion, so they can live life the way they really want to. You have incredible potential within you waiting to be tapped. You may just need some guidance, insight, and inspirational fuel to propel you in the right direction.

There was a time not long ago when I had no sense of fulfillment in my life, and I did not feel very good about myself. Life had gone from being able to do almost anything I wanted to do to being a huge financial bummer. The choices that came with financial freedom were gone, and the overwhelming weight of feeling stuck had mired me deeply in self-pity.

My focus for several years had been on finding the right business to turn life around. This self-focus and self-absorption led to losing an important relationship with someone who meant a great deal to me. The overall stress led to high cholesterol and high blood pressure. This unbalanced and negative mind-set caused me to be short-tempered and reactive, even with those special people closest to me. My sense of adventure had stagnated. The ski and beach adventures and exotic worldly trips were no more. My upbeat and happy self had disappeared, but where had it gone?

COURAGE to Find the FIRE Within is about sharing personal epiphanies, experiences, lessons, and insights that have allowed me to transform myself, develop an empowering mindset, and turn my life around. It's about sharing my passion with you to help you find your passion, so you can transform yourself and empower your life.

Within the past two years, life has completely turned around for me. Self-confidence is stronger than ever before. My mindset is such that I have absolute belief in my abilities and can see and feel the incredible potential within me. There is clarity for my passion. Focus and commitment are in force with a vengeance. My first book is here. My second book is written and going through editing.

My personal success coach told me I had a gift to help and inspire people. About 45 days later, I was presented with one of two annual recognition awards, the Servant Leadership Award, at an annual marketing event in Dallas. For me, there is no feeling in the world like helping someone realize they have tremendous potential inside of them and sharing insights with them so they can tap into it to get their fuse burning.

If you're prepared to commit and follow through with consistent focus and discipline, then get ready and get excited. Your life is about to change as you embark on the journey of a lifetime.

WHO I AM AND WHY I CAN HELP

Since you are reading this, it more than likely means you're at a point in your life where you're fed up with the pain and frustration of the way things are, and are serious about taking action to change your life. The quest of self-growth and the resulting transformation that occur takes focus, effort, consistency, patience, and hard work. With dedication it will be one of the most rewarding experiences of your life.

Progress only comes with change. Reflect on this for a few minutes. Children are growing and changing every day, beginning the moment they are born. Environment is a key factor for a child's development. Just as a plant must be nurtured and cared for consistently, providing a proper environment is essential for healthy growth. My hope is to provide insight and inspiration, so you can plant your own seed and learn how to nurture this life-transforming kernel to realize your inherent, true potential.

Becoming aware of your passions, strengths, weaknesses, and environment is essential. This not only involves your physical environment but the people in your life as well. Beginning with my story, I will share lessons, insights, and epiphanies, so you can relate, learn, and apply the principles of COURAGE to transform yourself and your life and begin to live by your own design.

There is a fiery passion deep within me to help others. Ironic as it may be, individuals can only be helped if they are absolutely serious about helping themselves. Once insights are learned and inspirational epiphanies occur, only by taking consistent, committed action will true transformation occur, allowing you to change your life in incredible ways.

Developing an empowering mind-set will lead you to see your true potential. This mind-set begins with a value that has completely changed my life—gratitude. Gratitude will allow you to see opportunity to grow in every situation.

What causes the trepidation, hesitation, procrastination, self-doubt, disbelief, and even the anger you feel, when you start feeling stuck, down, or depressed about aspects of your life? Fear.

What single value, when you are completely filled with it, leaves no room for fear? Gratitude.

Gratitude changes everything. Even during the most challenging and seemingly difficult times, it will directly empower you to find the hidden opportunities in these experiences. It could simply be a lesson. It could be realizing that your frustration is a result of being focused on yourself and not having awareness for the needs of others. When you learn how to bring an attitude of gratitude into your mind-set, it will change you. Gratitude will lead to more conscious, empowering actions that will change what happens next in amazing ways.

Sometimes there is a complete lack of gratitude or appreciation until we have lost something dear to us, such as a special relationship. Even developing gratitude afterwards is a wonderful thing, as it will open your eyes, heart, and mind for the future. It will keep you from being resentful, a fear-based and often consuming type of anger.

For several years, being completely self-absorbed and focused on what I thought I needed to do to turn my life around blinded me as to how extremely fortunate I had been during an almost eight-year relationship. There had been no awareness on my part for the needs of my beautiful girlfriend.

Finally, she was fed up and ended the relationship. Being tired of the seemingly endless arguments, this was fine with me at first. Then gratitude entered my life and completely changed my perspective. Upon reviewing a list I'd made with every characteristic and value I wanted and needed for my perfect soul mate, she met every single item. Wow, I'd really screwed up a potentially perfect relationship as a direct result of my complete lack of awareness and affection.

Gratitude allowed me to deal with the overwhelming sense of loss. I have learned huge, life-transforming lessons. Gratitude has led to an entirely new and improved version of myself. Never again will self-absorption take control. Rather, awareness and appreciation will fill my heart, eyes, mind, and soul. What an amazing and life-changing lesson and epiphany, simply gifts from gratitude.

Be grateful for the challenges in your life. Reflect on the opportunity within each and every challenge. By changing how you view past challenges (with frustration, anger, and resentment), you will change your future.

COURAGE to Find the FIRE Within has transformed from a dream into a reality as a result of my own commitment to realize my inherent potential. The formulation and strategy of the format and content stem from my own life's lessons leading to my ability to relate my life experiences, my mind-set, and my passion to help people move past their subconscious fear. Working on communication skills, becoming aware of the capacity to inspire, and being able to actually distinguish the difference between an experience from my standpoint and that of the person on the other end, was the spark to ignite this work.

You are obviously serious about learning concepts you can apply by taking action to change your life. Look into your very core and reflect on who you are now and where you are in your life. This is a very personal and often challenging quest. It is vital to create a bond of determined trust within yourself and develop the belief in yourself that is mandatory for success. You must define what success means to you. Be sure to write down your definition to make it real.

It is also important to build upon a foundation of trust between you (the reader) and me (the mentor or coach). This means I will express from my heart with passion and integrity. The irony of just having shared this with you is that trust and integrity cannot simply be stated— they must be earned and demonstrated. Integrity begins within and you must remain aware of it. When you make the commitment to take action and do not, you are out of integrity with yourself. It is vital to live in integrity with yourself. If you lose that, take personal responsibility, apologize to yourself, and get back on track.

The bottom line is that no matter how much information, insight, and knowledge are shared with you, you must be committed and consistently apply what you've learned to experience the transformation and change you so adamantly desire. Be sure to take the time to reflect on the key factors and takeaways and diligently do the work, so you can nurture your own seed of potential and experience the results.

You are encouraged to challenge the content...reflect on it. Have your own epiphanies. You must challenge yourself. You have the potential to rise to this challenge and to any challenge. You must begin to believe in yourself, discarding any self-doubt. Make sure you know the difference between the feelings of hope and the feelings of expectation. Hope is simply wishing for something. Expectation is a mind-set that will lead you to take action because you expect certain results. For example, if you only hope you will achieve your goals, it is not very likely you will. When you expect your goals to be attained, it is a result of doing the work to get there, and you will be excited to do the work. Reflect on the truly empowering difference.

Life is truly in an ever-evolving and transformational state because of what you have done up to this point. I am passionate and excited to continue this journey with you. It's time for you to resolutely commit to the journey to your ultimate destination. Fasten your seat belt and start your engine!

CHAPTER ONE

HOW I FOUND MY PASSION

As long as I can remember, I've been a dreamer. Many of my dreams have become a reality at some point in my life. Can you relate?

I built a dream home in Jackson Hole, Wyoming, and skied an average of over 50 days a year for 12 years. During three visits to Portillo, Chile, my skis have hit the slopes and my taste buds have truly been spoiled with every bite at the all-inclusive Hotel Portillo. Heli-skiing in the Chugach Mountains outside of Valdez, Alaska, was the most exciting, exhilarating, and downright scariest experience of my life. The fresh Alaskan king crab and oysters from Prince William Sound, accompanied by amazing people sharing incredible stories and fulfilling laughter after spending the day skiing in mid-thigh deep powder will never be forgotten during the seven-day adventure based at the Tsaina Lodge.

My toes have been caressed by the incredible sands of spectacular, sometimes remote, tropical beaches all over the world. My eyes have gazed upon amazing art and historical artifacts in the Louvre in Paris, the Topaki Palace in Istanbul, and many other world-class museums. A Greek island cruise enlightened me to the amazing culture, world-renowned history, friendly people, masterful Mediterranean dishes, and spectacular water and views of a past world. This list of dreams that have become an experienced reality goes on and on.

It's the ultimate shock when you're living a spectacular and fulfilling life, and then suddenly it's simply...gone.

Personal decisions worsened by the recent economic downturn (okay, depression) directly led to losing my money and therefore losing the freedom to live the adventuresome life so loved by me and my loved ones. Can you relate to losing the ability to do what you want to do, which then changes the person you thought you were? To cap it off, have you ever lost the financial wherewithal to help the causes that are most dear to your heart? Then you understand. It is no fun. In fact, it's rather depressing.

Passion for life and adventure runs deeply in my veins and in my soul. This has been evident my entire life. However having the courage to find the fire within me—my passion, my purpose, my mission—has been a longer, more lingering journey. A few jobs, several entrepreneurial efforts, and three multilevel marketing experiences summarize my past career in a nutshell.

So what inspired the passion for my present career and how was it discovered? Ah, let's return to my story to find out.

As you know from your history classes in grade school and high school, Greece has some of the world's most historical sites, such as Athens, the Parthenon, and Delphi. When you have the privilege to spend seven days island hopping on a private Greek island cruise, your eyes are opened to the true glory of the Greek people and their history. During this Mediterranean adventure, the ten of us on board the *Alexandria* visited and explored six small, incredibly beautiful Greek islands. After the cruise, there were three absolutely eye-opening and highly educational days spent experiencing the culture and learning some of the history of Istanbul, Turkey, before visiting the awe-inspiring ruins of Ephesus.

For seven straight years there were annual trips with my beautiful and inspirational love, Kathy, to tropical destinations and islands, mainly in the Caribbean, such as Virgin Gorda, St. Bart's, Harbour Island, and Long Island, just to mention a few. Mexico and Florida provided slightly less exotic travel adventures. Earlier in life, there were two cruises on a 400 foot sailboat, *WindSpirit*, including an 18-day odyssey, beginning in Madeira, Portugal, continuing through the Straits of Gibraltar, and ending up in Rome.

Spending five weeks based in a 400-plus-year-old stone farmhouse outside of St. Remy de Provence in southern France, was possibly a once-in-a-lifetime, incredible, cultural and historical experience. Delectable French cuisine, ruins, relaxing in the countryside, and wonderful French people, were all "normal" experiences during this extended vacation.

Along with the financial freedom to travel worldwide, having the ability to buy nice clothes and things for my family, and being able to help charities and others financially whenever desired is a wonderful feeling. As you can tell, my life has at times been blessed with the financial independence most people only dream about. It was my reality.

And this reality disappeared right before my eyes, as if in a bolt of lightning…it seemed that fast!

Being unsure of what to do next, I was filled with doubt and consumed by feeling overwhelmed. I felt completely stuck, bogged down in the muck of my own comfort rut. I've been comfortable with myself, or at least thought I was, and then had the bottom fall out as my biggest fears seemed to come alive. Can you relate to this feeling of complete self-doubt and being unsure not only about yourself, but about your future? You know, that place where even though things aren't the way you want, you're fearful about doing something different, so you become complacent. You don't take the actions you need to take to transform yourself and change your life. You do not commit to developing new habits, routines, and daily rituals to become the person you want to be, that you must be, to get to your destination.

When your self-confidence dwindles to next to nothing, you end up not believing in yourself. Believing in yourself is the vital foundation for self-refinement, realizing your potential and changing your life.

Most people unintentionally allow their mind-sets to be conditioned in extremely negative and self-defeating ways. My subconscious led me to believe that finding a suitable business was the answer. Have you ever spent more money on building a business opportunity than you made? For me, there were several, including multilevel marketing ventures, before the hard-core realization hit me that no specific business is the remedy.

My focus had been on making money. This resulted in remaining in the exact same spot, making no progress and ending up nowhere near where I really wanted to be or being any closer to becoming the person—the leader—I dreamt of being.

Being self-absorbed and focused on money led to my own "ruin." Money and some of the larger material items were gone, including my dream house in Jackson Hole, Wyoming, in 2006. The time and serious effort necessary to figure out my specific purpose and ultimate destination, what I really wanted and the person and leader I wanted to become, had been nonexistent. Frustration and unhappiness with my life and with myself were the main emotions flowing throughout my very core. Can you relate to this from any point in your life?

When you don't know what to do, you tend to feel helpless and lost, not knowing where to begin to make your life better. When you are subconsciously focused on your fears, you likely have no clue about the existing, incredible potential lying within you that is waiting to be tapped and brought to life by your commitment and subsequent actions.

This was when the avalanche of epiphany hit me: many things and people in my life had been taken for granted, including the most all-around incredible woman I had ever met. My eyes were opened to the importance of taking personal responsibility for how my actions directly led to what happened in my life. The two values of gratitude and personal responsibility have had a truly life-changing impact.

This may seem crazy to you, but I wouldn't change any of the negative, horrible experiences I've gone through. Seriously!

You can't change the past. It is important to realize your choices and experiences have led to where you are today. Looking back with gratitude on these times led me to learn and grow, which changed my actions from that point forward.

If you do not feel fulfilled with where you are today, you can consciously choose to develop awareness of your true, inner potential and begin to take specific action to become the person, the leader, you dream about becoming to begin to live the way you really want to live.

My passions are my daughter, family, friends, staying fit, being active, traveling, skiing, playing tennis, seeking adventure, reading, writing, pursuing self-transformation, and inspiring others. This last passion has directly led to what you are reading now. Having a variety of passions has truly made life so enjoyable, exciting, inspiring, eye opening, and transformational. It's absolutely life changing when you know your passions, those things that fill you with excitement and get your adrenaline flowing. When you allow fear to take over, it extinguishes the flame of your passion.

The burning desire to be in control of my own life has led to several entrepreneurial endeavors. The present journey really began when the recent economic crash descended upon us about seven years ago. In hindsight, it's not a pleasurable experience to become deeply entrenched in a rut, to be in a place where your fears are in charge, causing you to be in a constant reactionary state. When you're completely focused on making money, it usually results in the feeling of riding the hamster wheel of life, going nowhere fast.

My favorite saying is: "If your life is full of challenges and problems, if things aren't going the way you want, then it's time to look in the mirror. There you'll see the cause…and the solution." (I call this "The Man in the Mirror.") There is a ton of irony when you have known and quoted a saying for a long time and then suddenly realized you have not been applying it. For me it was a matter of looking in the mirror and saying, "Hello? Anyone home?"

A famous quote often attributed to Albert Einstein is, "Insanity is doing the same thing over and over again and expecting different results."

It's never too late to realize that you have incredible potential within you and to ask yourself if you know your purpose. The next steps are to (1) figure out what you want and where you want to be, (2) know where you are now, and (3) develop and design a plan of action to get you from here to there. Tony Robbins calls this a Massive Action Plan or MAP.

Almost all of the challenges in your life have been caused by one person—you. At first, this can be a very disheartening self-realization, almost depressing. When you change your perspective by recognizing the solution has been there all along, let the excitement begin to flow through your very core. One of the biggest epiphanies in life is that in order to get what you really want, it's time to get to work on yourself and realize your goals.

If you are committed to having the courage to find the fire within and to discovering your passion, you must begin by resolutely committing to doing the work to transform yourself and developing an awareness of your passion, the origin of your inspiration, your fears, and your ultimate desires.

This journey begins with reconditioning your mind-set. Success, whatever it means to you, begins with believing in yourself. Skill-sets to cultivate include focus, discipline, and the ability to keep distractions to a minimum. It's vital to have clarity about exactly what it is you want, so you can figure out the actions you need to take to make progress to your ultimate destination.

When you become aware of gratitude and choose it to be a foundational value in your life, it will transform you and how you look at every situation and relationship. Gratitude allows you to see opportunity, even in circumstances you don't like. It will change your life as it did mine. It is absolutely eye opening to know you will never again take anything or anyone for granted and to be able to see the opportunity to learn and grow from every experience.

When you discover your passion and inspiration, you can stop focusing on your fears and begin to have gratitude for your newfound ability to focus on what it is you really want. It's time to make a resolute commitment to start the journey to transform yourself and subsequently, your life. If you don't think you're ready for this, it's a sign of self-doubt. You must construct a new and empowering mind-set. Without taking action, you will never make progress toward your goals.

This new combination of having a truly self-empowering mind-set and taking action will begin an incredible adventure. Every time you achieve your goals and arrive at a new milestone, the feeling of accomplishment will further inspire you, and your momentum will gain more traction. You will know it's time to set new goals, and your self-confidence will grow stronger.

Sure, there will be times when you may feel stuck or overwhelmed. These warning signs mean it's time to get back on the bike, so to speak, and continue pedaling, to keep taking focused and directed action. Life-changing epiphanies will begin to pop into your head more regularly, altering not only how you look at things, but more importantly, how you deal with them. You will begin to be proactive, instead of continuing to practice the subconscious habit of being reactive. When you choose to continue your evolution, it will be completely self-empowering. When combined with patience, great things will start to happen…they're still happening for me!

When people start reaching out to you for help, for inspiration, or to say "thank you" for making a difference in their lives, there is a deeper, more meaningful message to which you need to pay attention. When individuals reach out to you, you are being recognized for a skill-set or a strength you have. For me, this was a revelation that I had the ability to reflect on what I've learned from my own experiences and recognize my innermost passion, and use it to inspire others. This is precisely how *COURAGE to Find the FIRE Within* became a reality. It was destined to be shared with the world.

So, what does it mean to be inspired to look for the courage to find the "fire" within you? Fire is your passion, your purpose, your mission, your why, your inspiration. It's whatever fills you with pure adrenaline, energy, and excitement. It's what gets you out of bed first thing in the morning, filled with excited anticipation to achieve your goals and to make a difference, to leave your mark on the world. Figuring out your passion may truly be one of the most worthwhile actions you will ever take during your life.

Finding the fire within you takes resolute commitment. It takes effort. It means opening your eyes, heart, mind, and soul to the incredible potential within you. It means crafting a new, inspirational mind-set, one where you have absolute belief in yourself.

The percentage ranges, but sources indicate that approximately 96 percent of the world's population are stuck in their own entrapped mind-sets, not believing they have the potential or ability to do what it takes to change their lives. Are you committed to being one of the four percent and change your life forever? Take several slow, deep breaths and commit to doing what it takes to transform yourself, so you can change your life from this point forward. Write this commitment down to make it real—right now. Seriously, don't read on until you write it down. If you're reading this, you're definitely not driving, so pick up a pen and spend a few minutes to set your commitment in ink! Read your written commitment out loud to yourself every day to begin to recondition your mind-set.

Tony Robbins, the world-famous motivational guru, tells you in *Get the Edge: A 7-Day Program to Transform Your Life* to never leave the site of setting a goal without taking at least one small action toward that goal. If you're not familiar with Tony's incredible work resulting from over 30 years of commitment and passion, you will enjoy listening to this dynamic audio program or any of Tony's transformational works.

I'm here to support you; you can reach out to me personally (www.peterhobler.com). Know that ultimately, it's up to you to commit and to take the necessary action. The majority of people in this world simply do what they think they are supposed to do for their career. They have no idea how to figure out their source of inspiration so they can live life with passion. They may take the time to learn, yet they do not make the commitment to apply the new knowledge into their lives. It's the combination of knowledge plus action that leads to true empowerment.

Your life is waiting for you as an amazing, exciting, and extremely fulfilling journey. I am passionate and excited to inspire you, to help you figure out your passion so you can begin your own unique, life-transforming journey.

As the Nike slogan says…"Just Do It!"

Taking that first step of action is essential to your success.

CHAPTER TWO

THE FIRE WITHIN YOU

Just what exactly is the FIRE within you? It's your potential, your passion, your purpose, your mission, your vision, your *why*. It is ignited and fueled by the embers of the very things that get your adrenaline pumping and energy flowing in a way that fills you with inspiration, fulfillment, happiness, and joy.

You have everything inside of you right now to make your ultimate destination a reality: to get what you really want, to be where you want to be, and to become the person (the leader) you dream of being. The foundation for your success can be boiled down to a single, self-empowering asset. It is the very basis on which you will be able to create and build the stepping-stones to get you to your destination.

Mind-set is what will make you or break you. It is your desires, your commitment, and your gratefulness for the opportunity in every situation. It is up to you to develop the mind-set of absolute belief in yourself: to choose your course of action and be who you want to be. Combining your purpose and passion with this belief will lead you to your ultimate destination.

Why do so many people feel defeated, helpless, or give up when they think they've "failed"? It's a result of prior conditioning, like thinking you can never do anything right when things don't go the way you want them to. Feelings of being overwhelmed often consume people. It is the combination of having a huge list of things to do and the fear of not knowing exactly what to do in order to get things done and get what you want. Think about this. If you don't take personal responsibility for where you are, how are you ever going to change things so you can get to where you want to be?

Are you wondering how to change your present mind-set? Just as for a sport or hobby you are passionate about, it's about learning skills, practicing, and conditioning. This begins with the awareness of your current mind-set. (Chapter 8 will share an exercise called "The Blame, Shame, Justify Game" that will open your eyes to the condition of your mind-set so you can see if it is empowering or self-defeating.) Then you must learn about concepts to practice, to nurture and strengthen your newfound, self-empowering mind-set.

If you find yourself doubting this, you need to immediately check in with yourself. Be aware what you think and say emanates energy that will bring you these very things into your life. Think about this. What is it you really want? Write it down now.

Did you write it down? If not, stop and do it to make it real, right now. This is a foundational starting point for your personal transformation and journey to success. Whether you believe it or not there is incredible potential inside of you waiting to be unleashed.

This is your innate potential. Some might describe this to be your God-given potential. Our culture, experiences, and environment often combine to mold and condition us in doubtful, disbelieving ways, all of which stem from fear. Have you ever said, "I could never do that"? Whatever it is, why would you think this, much less say such a statement? What is it inside of you that resulted in such disbelief, making you think you can't do something…much less anything?

It's fear. It's usually a deeply embedded subconscious fear that has been conditioned over time. Could it be as a child your parents constantly scolded you and told you that you could not do something? Maybe you always heard that you could not afford something you wanted to own or that you wanted to do. Over time, this becomes your subconscious mindset of disbelief. Think how disempowering this is for your future.

What has been holding you back, those stifling obstacles concealed in the dark realm of your subconscious fears? The bottom line is that the results you get are up to you. No one can really help you unless you are absolutely committed to helping yourself. This means you are filled with a resonating, fiery passion and resolutely committed to reaching your destination, doing the work, taking personal responsibility, holding yourself accountable, and following through with consistent action.

It's true you have inherent potential inside of you to do pretty much whatever you want. If you find yourself doubting this, it should be an "aha!" moment regarding your mind-set. To experience true self-transformation, you must definitively be dedicated to work diligently and consistently so you can refine yourself to be the passionate leader who's inside of you. You must learn to be open-minded and apply and practice what you've learned.

You are now prepared, ready to take the leap into the realm of the astonishing journey of self-transformation, or as JT DeBolt, Mission Accomplishment Expert, would more aptly say, your journey of self-refinement. After all, the potential is already there, so you're redefining and refining yourself to realize your potential.

Make sure you're absolutely committed, open-minded, focused, and patient. You will begin to feel and see remarkable transformational signs of self-growth. Things will start to happen in your life as a direct result of your new and empowering mind-set combined with your commitment, gratitude, and consistent, focused action.

Embrace the challenges ahead of you. Be grateful for them, for you must go through challenges to experience growth and transformation. Commit to having the courage to find your FIRE, to develop your Focus, know your Inspiration, take Responsibility, and have consistent Excellence to being your best self. What you feel, think, and do will determine your future.

CHAPTER THREE

THE ELEMENTS OF FIRE

How do you go about finding your own personal inspiration and figuring out your purpose, your mission, your vision, your *why*? Once you figure out your *why*, how do you start taking passionate action to achieve your goals and live life the way you want?

It's exhilarating and life changing to figure out what it is that fills you with passion, what it is that drives you to take action. This could be a direct result of being fed up with experiencing the pain and suffering from things and situations you do not want in your life any longer. Maybe it's inspiration stemming from something that will bring you immense pleasure in the future, such as reaching your ultimate destination and being able to have the financial and time freedom to do the things you've always dreamed of, such as spending four months a year on a wonderful remote tropical island. It could be an amazing individual who inspires you.

Whatever the source of your inspiration, you must be serious and resolutely committed to transforming yourself if you really intend to change your life. If you're not absolutely committed, then you will never be included in the rare breed of those who actually achieve their goals and realize their dreams. These are the self-made thoroughbreds, the determined and passionate 3 to 4 percent, who commit to finding the courage to find their fire to live their personal version of success.

These self-made leaders have qualities and values that have been developed and honed consistently over time. Success is not automatic and this 4 percent or less of the world's population knows it. They courageously welcome the challenge and seize the opportunity to learn and grow with each situation, no matter how difficult. They are aware of their innermost subconscious fears and are resolute in their commitment to take *action* to move past them. They will not be deterred or denied.

They do not know failure. There really is no such thing as failure. Every step along the path is viewed as an opportunity to learn and grow. A step in the wrong direction will still serve them, as they will not make the same choices again. They will develop strong, finely honed skill-sets which will take them to success.

What is it that drives them? What is it that keeps them from becoming one of the typical "quitters" when the going gets tough? It's a force within that has been ignited by either pain or pleasure. Both are extremely powerful and driving motivators.

People often subconsciously let pain consume them. Because they are so focused on their pain, the consequence is defeat. They quit taking consistent action and end up living in despair and unhappiness. Moaning, groaning, and constant complaining is their modus of operation.

Having to choose between pleasure and pain in the present moment can be a huge distraction and has deterred even some of the strongest off their journey to success. This is because so many make the immediate choice of pleasure, which means they don't do the work and therefore do not reap the rewards and experience even greater pain later due to their lack of focus and self-discipline.

Reaching the brink and being fed up with the pain of your life can be used to ignite the initial spark of fire inside you. Knowing your pleasure-filled ultimate destination with clarity, where you want to be in life, what you want, and who you want to be can also cause combustion of the heartfelt potential FIRE within you!

Using the combination of pain and pleasure can be unstoppable when you have discovered your genuine and profound source of inspiration. The starting point is knowing you're done with the pain of the past that's led to your present situation and having complete clarity for your destination. You know where you are and you know where you want to be. Now you can figure out how to get from here...to there.

So, just how do you accomplish this? I am so glad you asked!

Forging the fire within means developing and conditioning new habits and skill-sets to ignite and hone the four elements of FIRE so you can live life with passion:

Focus. Inspiration. Responsibility. Excellence.

Once you begin your fiery journey, you will begin to experience personal transformation through your self-refinement (I prefer this over self-improvement as you have now recognized your own inner potential and are taking action to fulfill it). Your goals and even your destination may change as you become more enlightened and more "self-refined". So now you may be wondering how the four elements of fire come together so what you really want can actually become your reality...

FOCUS

You must know what to *focus* on. Visualize your destination, the place where you want to be, what you want, and the person you want to be. See it. Feel it. Taste it. Know it intimately and with clarity. Develop your mind-set as if you are already there.

There is more than one way to figure out your goals and the specific action steps that will lead you to your destination. It's vital to *focus* on the process, the prioritized actions you must take consistently in order to make progress.

Know it's not any specific business or job that makes you successful. It's working on yourself, building your leadership skills and your skill-sets. This equates to continual self-education and self-refinement, whether it be from experience, learning from a mentor, taking a class, or reading a book.

INSPIRATION

Determine what truly inspires you, what drives you. The origin of your inspiration is the main fuel to drive you to tap into your innermost potential that already exists deep within your soul. This is your purpose, your *why*. Why do you want to reach your ultimate destination?

Be aware when you are reacting to your subconscious fears. Fear is the biggest barrier to success. It causes people to react with anger, hesitation, trepidation, procrastination, self-doubt, and disbelief. It will emanate a highly negative energy, which attracts the same type of energy in return. This is definitely not what you want to do.

If you are not aware of your fears, they can consume you and completely take control of your life. I call this the "vicious cycle of subconscious fear." What you focus on is what you get back. This is a major foreshadowing epiphany for what you will attract in your life. Knowing this, focus on your inspiration!

There is one value that when you're filled with it completely, it leaves no room for fear. This will be life transforming for you. If you think you know what it is, write it down now and compare notes near the end of the book to see if you were right. Don't look now. It will make more sense if you wait.

RESPONSIBILITY

Taking personal responsibility is huge. No one can be responsible for your commitment to consistently take action…except *you*! You must learn and take action to apply, be productive, hold yourself accountable, track your performance, and have patience.

Taking personal responsibility is rooted in integrity. Integrity begins within any given individual. It is not something you can say you have. Like trust, it must be consistently demonstrated and earned. In order to expect someone else to have integrity while interacting with you, you must likewise operate on the foundation of core integrity. Ethics, morals, and values all come into play here.

Without integrity, it is impossible to provide ultimate value to others to build trust, the foundation on which the most successful and innovative entrepreneurs in the world anchor themselves to build a meaningful and attractive reputation.

EXCELLENCE

Life goes by quickly. Our time on this planet is indeed short. Here are three related questions to ask while looking in the mirror each day. The responses will impact your life.

Did I do my best today?

Was I my best self?

Why am I here? (Also a great question to ask when you're not being focused and disciplined!).

To be your best self, you must understand that you indeed have incredible potential, become aware of your fears, and totally believe in yourself. This new conditioning is a direct result of your daily mind-set work. It emanates from your thought processes, language, and actions.

Excellence stems from knowing when you're reacting to your fears and making the conscious choice to be grateful for the opportunity in every situation and circumstance, even the ones you really don't like. (This is an example of the perfect time to ask yourself, "Why am I here?"). When you are filled with gratitude, it will leave no room for the fear and you will be able to take action directly leading to progress toward your goals. This is the springboard to changing how you operate, that is, how you make decisions and take subsequent action.

Being your best means releasing any and all negative energy from your past that has built up so you can clear the path to receiving as a result of the value you will soon be providing to the world. It means honing your self-awareness so you know when you're blaming, shaming, or justifying, whether of yourself or of someone else. Admit when you've made a mistake and take targeted action to fix it.

Now you can focus on developing a truly inspirational mindset to propel you forward as you commit to take action to find the FIRE within, so you can live passionately the way you want to live.

CHAPTER FOUR

THE 7 PRINCIPLES OF COURAGE

There are seven principles of COURAGE to learn and apply so you can build the mind-set and skill-sets to recondition yourself and form the four elements of FIRE that will empower you. These will help you build and condition new habits to get to where you really want to be.

Before embarking on the journey ahead of you, first reflect on the incredible, untapped potential lying within you. Everyone has tremendous potential. They have simply never realized this or more importantly, never believed it. Awareness is such an interesting facet of life. Without it, it's as though our eyes and our minds are closed tight. Let me share an example.

I once asked a dear friend of mine if he would like to fly first class on a trip we were planning. My friend replied, "No."

I came back with, "If money was no object, why not?"

The reply that came back opened my eyes. He said, "I just don't have the desire to fly first class."

I asked him, "Have you ever flown first class?"

My friend responded, "No."

I shared my epiphany with him, saying, "Now, I understand your answer. I have flown first class. Once you've flown up front, you never want to sit in the back again."

We don't know what we don't know. Profound, isn't it?

In order to be able to get from where you are today to where you want to be, you must understand where you are now and look at what has led you to this place. You must be able to take personal responsibility for the actions you have taken that led you to where you are now. Next, you must have clarity of your destination: where you want to be in life, what you want, and who you want to be.

COURAGE PRINCIPLE 1: CLARITY OF DESTINATION

If you don't know where you're going, you'll never get there! Clarity of Destination provides insights to forge your FIRE Element 1, Focus. Having awareness of yourself, your environment, what inspires you, and what you focus on is essential. This will passionately empower you to make progress and to ultimately get to your destination.

COURAGE PRINCIPLE 2: ORIGIN OF INSPIRATION

Figuring out your source of inspiration is vital. This is what gets your adrenaline going and fills you with passion. It brings Focus and Inspiration together, which can lead you to knowing your purpose and passion.

Sources of inspiration include people, books, experiences, causes, love, or even the majestic wonder of nature (which so many people take for granted). In other words, by observing the examples people set, absorbing mind-opening information, learning from life, impacting people's lives, enjoying your family, and admiring the endless, awe-inspiring aspects of nature, you can discover electrifying sources of inspiration. Sometimes this may simply mean sitting still in nature to quiet your mind, taking time to reflect and observe, and opening your heart, mind, and soul.

COURAGE PRINCIPLE 3: UNREALIZED POTENTIAL

Without recognizing you have unrealized and incredible potential, you won't be inspired to develop the mind-set to maintain your determination, drive, and commitment. Believing in yourself is essential. When you know you can accomplish your goals, you will be empowered to overcome any challenge by doing what it takes.

Where these come together is in the conditioning of new habits, rituals, and routines. It's about realizing how reacting to fears is actually the biggest obstacle to your success. It's about belief, confidence, focus, and discipline. (When you bring COURAGE Principle 6 into your life, there is no room for fear. This is huge!).

COURAGE PRINCIPLE 4: RESPONSIBILITY

Taking personal responsibility for the actions that have led you to where you are now and for developing your plan of action is a life altering and most important step. Find a mentor or coach to guide you and provide insight to set up some form of structure and a self-nurturing environment.

Responsibility begins with the person in the mirror. It's about realizing that you are where you are because of your prior actions. It's all about understanding that in order to get to where you really want to be, it's up to you and only you! It's about the epiphany you must have that it's time to take personal responsibility and uncork your potential by inventing a new you and taking consistent action. Without the element of Responsibility, there is no action, no accountability, no productivity, no consistency, and therefore no progress toward achieving your goals and getting to your destination.

COURAGE PRINCIPLE 5: AWARENESS

It's vital to be aware of what's holding you back. The biggest obstacle to success is fear. Fear causes anger, resentment, worry, procrastination, trepidation, self-doubt, disbelief, even depression. Having the awareness that what you focus on is what you get is a major epiphany. When you're subconsciously operating from a place of fear, in any form, this is what you will get more of. Is this what you want—the "vicious cycle of subconscious fear"?

When you know your destination and focus on the process for accomplishing your goals, this will be what you get more of. Isn't this exactly what you want?

COURAGE PRINCIPLE 6: GRATITUDE

Gratitude is a life-changing value. When you can see the opportunity in every situation and circumstance, even those that would normally drain all of your energy because you can't stand it, you will be ultimately empowered! Gratitude allows you to change how you view the past. It will empower you to be conscious, appreciative, and proactive.

Why? Because when you are filled with gratitude there is no room for fear. What you do next will be very different as you will be operating from a place of empowerment, not a place of paralyzing fear.

COURAGE PRINCIPLE 7: EXCELLENCE

Excellence solidifies the process of your fiery evolution, forging the four elements of your FIRE. Being your best self will produce a bluish-white flame that will allow you to hone the elements of FIRE and will launch you into a new realm, one that will conceivably blow your mind as things begin to happen beyond your wildest dreams. Excellence is what brings everything to a fiery culmination of combustion that leads to momentum.

One of the biggest ironies is that you will find further and deeper inspiration when momentum starts. As you begin to achieve your goals and make progress toward your ultimate destination, you will have further insights, epiphanies and empowerment. Some of your desires, your purpose, even your destination may change. Why?

Transformation is what life is all about. As we learn and grow, we transform. As a result, what we want may change. This is wonderful! This is what it's all about!

Are you ready to get on with it? I can hardly stand the excitement! Take a big breath…Feel it…breathe in….hold it for three counts…now breathe out…three counts.

Now, turn the page for COURAGE Principle 1…

CHAPTER FIVE

PRINCIPLE 1: CLARITY OF DESTINATION

If we could first know where we are, and whither we are tending, we could then better judge what to do, and how to do it.
– Abraham Lincoln

In order to make progress toward something, you must know what it is that you are working towards. In this case, I am talking about your ultimate destination. Where do you want to be, what do you want, and who do you want to be? In what time frame do you want to get to your destination?

These vital points of information will be used to figure out how you will get from here, where you are now, to there, where you want to be. This will become your plan of action. There are many acronyms for this. Tony Robbins calls it your Massive Action Plan. It could also be called your Life Plan or Success Plan.

I focused on making money for several years and never achieved my goals. Once I started focusing on my passions and my destination (what I could do with my money, such as going on a mission trip every year and being able to buy a new house), I began making progress rather quickly. The irony is, once my focus switched, money started flowing in.

Becoming aware of your strengths and focusing on your purpose, your passion, and your destination, is an empowering combination. If you don't know exactly what you want, but you absolutely know you are not where you want to be, that's okay. You can figure out your strengths and weakness and then your destination and the specific actions you will need to take to get there. You have some work to do to prepare yourself, to develop your courage.

If you know exactly what you want and who you want to be, that is fantastic. You are ahead of the game. The next step is to figure out your strengths and weaknesses and the specific actions you need to take to become that person, the leader you must be to get to your destination. With the proper mindset and attitude, you will find tremendous opportunity in the work you will be doing. It will open your mind to your potential and the endless possibilities that lie ahead of you.

As you delve headfirst into learning and applying these concepts, you will start attracting like-minded people. Progress will be made as you begin to achieve your stepping-stone goals, and new doors of opportunity will open. You may discover new passions and strengths you didn't realize you had. Your inspiration will not only be renewed, but your energy will begin to feel much more empowering. It's an empowering feeling to achieve your goals and feel your inspiration soar and your commitment solidify.

As you do the exercises, always write them down. This makes your thoughts real. They are now a part of reality, a part of the universe. Keep a journal. In the future, you can revisit your thoughts and get a true understanding of where you once were and how much you have progressed. If you don't know exactly what you want, here are some thought provoking exercises to help you figure this out.

Write a list of what it is in your life that fills you with passion.

- Is it activities, sports, hobbies, people, travel, a specific place?
- Is it art, culture, history, nature, water?
- Is it helping people in a general way or in a specific way?
- Is it being involved with your family, friends, or another group of people?
- What can't you do enough that always makes you feel fulfilled?

Think about what you're doing when your energy is the highest.

- What is it you could do for hours on end?
- What makes you feel happy, joyful, content?
- Where in life have you had the most success?

- What things have you been really good at?
- What seems effortless to you?
- What makes you feel happy and fulfilled?

If you're still finding it challenging to come up with answers, then go to a quiet place outside. Close your eyes and start taking slow, deep breaths. Breathe from your belly, not your diaphragm. Smile, even if you don't feel like it. It will change your energy. Take yourself to a mentally and emotionally peaceful place.

Now go through the process again, with focused and thoughtful reflection.

If you're still stuck, go ask five people who know you the best what they think makes you happy. Use their responses as a starting point. The main point of this exercise is to start opening your mind and your awareness as to what stirs your passion from deep inside. If you're like me, there is a chance that until this point you may not have spent much time reflecting on your passions, your purpose, your *why*, or even just what really fills you with excitement and makes you happy.

You have begun the process; you have now opened the floodgates of possible passions to begin flowing. The energy has started and you will be able to figure it out. Even if you already know your destination, you can discover further insights into your passions and open up more facets of your destination. As you learn, apply, and transform, your passion and your destination may begin to change as well. This is all part of your transformational journey as you go through the transformational process of self-refinement .

CHAPTER SIX

COURAGE PRINCIPLE 2: ORIGIN OF INSPIRATION

Cherish your visions and your dreams as they are the children of your soul, the blueprints of your ultimate achievements.
– Napoleon Hill

True inspiration fills you with passion, excitement, and focused energy. It leads you to take action. When you know the origin of your inspiration, you can consciously choose to focus on it to drive yourself, to motivate yourself. Inspiration is a key to your dreams.

Do you feel inspired? Have you ever wondered where inspiration comes from? What is your source of inspiration? What drives you? What fills you with passion, excitement, and the desire to take action? Do you even have a clue? If not, that's okay. I had been conditioned all of my life to deal with each day as it came. I did not know what inspired me. I did not have any idea of the limitless potential being held prisoner deep within the confines of my subconscious fears. I did not have a plan of action.

Inspiration is found in many ways: from books, from music, from experiences, from people. You might feel inspired when you think of something you are truly committed to achieving, such as your ultimate destination. Maybe the source of your inspiration is a cause you passionately support. It could be your children. My personal inspiration emanates from several sources, including the most influential individual to have ever been a part of my life.

My brother, Chris, was eight years younger than me. From a very young age, he passionately pursued his dream of being a musician. He had his own original rock band, Sonic Joyride, and his own record label, Anomaly Records. He wrote the music, sang lead vocals, and played lead guitar. He learned how to be a sound engineer and a producer in the studio when the band was recording. Music was one of my brother's biggest sources of inspiration.

Sonic Joyride was beginning to make real progress in one of the most competitive and challenging industries. The band purchased a used school bus and turned it into a traveling sound stage, which they named The Cosmic Sled. There was a 20,000-watt sound system in the belly of the bus. Two huge, high-quality speakers were built into the right side of the *Cosmic Sled* with waterproof doors that were opened for performances. There were basic handcrafted bunk beds in the back of the bus (which I helped build), and a refrigerator had been installed. To top off this original traveling music sideshow, there was a stage welded on top of the bus with a lid that could be propped up and used as a video screen in the background. The band could pull up anywhere in the *Cosmic Sled* and be set up and performing within 10 to 15 minutes. This was quite an astonishing feat for any live musical performance.

In the late 1990s and early 2000s, Sonic Joyride went on a U.S. national tour and made CNN Headline news, MTV news, and more. I believe they got a ticket for disturbing the peace when they pulled up and performed impromptu outside of The David Letterman Show in New York City! Sonic Joyride was making progress with their music and had an ever growing fan base. Chris was completely inspired and living his dream with passion.

Suddenly, at age 34, Chris was diagnosed with Amyotrophic Lateral Sclerosis (ALS), also known as Lou Gehrig's disease. His inspiration and passion quickly and dramatically morphed from music to saving not only his life but to helping save lives of other individuals with neurological diseases.

Chris started the public charity Hope Happens for Neurological Disorders in 2001 and subsequently came up with the concept for one of the first collaborative research laboratories in the world. The Hope Center for Neurological

Disorders is a collaborative effort between Hope Happens and the Washington University Neurological Department, which officially opened its doors on November 1, 2004. Today, The Hope Center employs over 90 full-time scientists and has raised close to $40 million to date. The Hope Center has had major research breakthroughs in Alzheimer's and Parkinson's diseases so far.

Chris realized that 20 years after our maternal grandfather died from ALS in September 1981, there had been no progress in the research for cures. In fact, this type of research was almost nonexistent. He wanted to understand why.

It turned out that because only 30,000 people a year are diagnosed with ALS and almost all of them die within a very short period of time, there was no profit motivation for the bio techs, pharmaceuticals, drug companies, or even in the world of academia. These huge entities were more concerned with protecting their intellectual property because of the possible major financial gains in the future. Chris committed to change this and took the profit motivation out of his visionary equation.

The Hope Center for Neurological Disorders shares laboratory space, equipment, and all research approaches, analysis, and discoveries. There are a lot of similarities between neurological disorders, and Chris's idea was that though targeted research may not help a specific neurological disease, it could very well help another one. He even drafted legislation he submitted to the Missouri state government to encourage investment in neurological disease research.

My brother lost his amazingly determined and inspirational battle against the heinous disease of ALS on February 16, 2005. His incredible story and spirit live on via his inspirational vision, which still impacts the lives of others seven-and-a-half years after his passing.

Chris was my best friend as well as my brother. I miss him every day. His wonderful, loving wife and four incredible children miss him as a loving and committed husband and father every day. I recently hung Chris's portrait in my office, and when I feel the need for inspiration, I look at him, talk to him, and reach out to him. The challenges he faced make mine seem more than miniscule.

Chris had his musical dreams, which were getting so close to reality, stolen away in an instant. His ability to move gradually disappeared over the next two years. The once-gifted athlete and passionate, focused, and extremely talented musician was no more. All of his abilities resulting from the effort and time he had put into developing his tremendous skills for playing the guitar and singing vanished.

His incredible attitude regarding his innermost potential never wavered. His talents, creativity, and intelligence now had a new opportunity to rise to the surface to flourish, so he could impact the world. He felt inspired to redirect and channel his passion and energy to raise funds and awareness to combat neurological disorders. His drive to bring his concept for making collaborative research to being a laboratory reality will forever be awe-inspiring to me. My brother set one of the most courageous examples I have ever seen. He was even somehow able to maintain his sense of humor until the bittersweet end.

My brother's mission was, and still is, inspiring and contagious. Though he is gone, his inspiration and his incredible efforts are still making a difference in the world. To get more information about Hope Happens for Neurological Disorders, go to www.hopehappens.org. You will also find a direct link to The Hope Center for Neurological Disorders. If you have a family member or friend with a neurological disorder, go to www.facebook.com/shoutoutforhope and post a memorial video and use your personal story to "Shout Out" and spread the word of hope.

Chris faced the insurmountable obstacles of not being able to physically move (except from the neck up) and not being able to speak. A communications software program called "Dasher" enabled him to communicate and use his computer. He had to have someone move him or do things that we take for granted. His mind was incapable of communicating via his motor neurons with his voluntary muscles. Yet his inspiration, passion, and commitment led him to impact the world. Chris Hobler created an amazing and inspiring legacy, one that will continue well into the future as it impacts the lives of not only individuals with neurological disorders, but their families, friends, caregivers, and scientific researchers.

Writing this all-too-brief summary of my brother's story to provide inspiration for you has led me to a life-changing epiphany. I've asked myself, (the Man in the Mirror), okay, so what's my excuse? I can move and speak. What's holding me back from taking action to fuel my inspirational fire and follow my passion?

CHRIS HOBLER
Father, husband, brother, friend, source of inspiration.
True Hero.

Above: Chris with daughter Ella.

Below: Chris on his wedding day with his dog Aslan.

My questions to you are: What's your excuse? What fears are holding you back? What's your life-changing inspiration? What's your passion? How committed are you to finding the answers to these questions?

Another source of inspiration for me is my daughter, Alie. I want to set the best possible example for her and teach her the values of integrity, goal setting, focus, discipline, hard work, personal responsibility, and gratitude so she can live her dreams. I love her beyond measure.

My former better half, Kathy, inspires me in many ways. I so wanted to be able to provide, express, and share life's adventures with her, so we could magnify our desires and experiences together.

I am inspired to begin to realize my own true, innermost potential. I have a deeply embedded passion to wake people up and inspire them to have courage to find the fire within, so they can live life passionately the way they want. Everyone has extraordinary potential inside, including you. Your courage, commitment, and inspiration are the keys to opening the door to your realm of possibility.

There is often irony beneath the surface. Each time we achieve major goals and realize a new level of personal potential, we subsequently must set new goals to reach an even higher level of potential. For those of us resolutely committed to realizing our fullest potential, this is an ongoing journey of fulfillment.

I am inspired, determined, committed, and it is one of my greatest passions to inspire you by setting the example, by having recognized my own potential and having raised the bar of my own personal expectations and standards. I am grateful for the opportunity every day brings—every situation and every challenge—to grow and transform, to broaden my horizons and to tap into my potential and get it consistently flowing so I can live life the way I want.

What is the origin, the source of your inspiration?

Think about who and what is important to you. Family? Maybe you have a cause that fills you with passion, a cause for individuals who are not as fortunate. Do you have a specific dream you've thought about your entire life but never believed was possible until now?

Be clear and know that money is *not* a source of inspiration. It is about what the money can do or provide for you, but it's not the actual money. Money is merely the vehicle. It is vitally important to understand this distinction. Focus on what you want, on what inspires you and on the process, the actions.

Think about what you've done in the past where you've felt the excitement and energy flow through you? What have you enjoyed doing? What gives you a true feeling of fulfillment? What things fill you with passion?

With some focused inner reflection and by doing the work, you can and will figure out your passion, your inspiration. Know that anything worthwhile takes effort. Your ultimate destination will not come to you. You must do what it takes to get there.

So, how do you get to the point where you recognize the unrealized potential deep within you so you can develop the courage to find the fire within you, and figure out your passion and purpose?

CHAPTER SEVEN

COURAGE PRINCIPLE 3: UNREALIZED POTENTIAL = MIND-SET

Some day I shall be President.
–Abraham Lincoln

Life-changing potential lies within everyone. Unfortunately, most people are unaware that their culture and environment have conditioned them to be completely oblivious to their own uniquely empowering potential. Being unaware of their unrealized potential becomes the foundation for how they live their life.

From a young age, people are often told they cannot do certain things or that they will never be able to afford the nicer things in life, sometimes even basic things, such as a car. Constantly hearing "There's no way you can do that…" negatively conditions them over time and develops a poverty mind-set, which then becomes their reality. One of life's biggest mysteries is why more individuals do not "wake up and smell the coffee," as my daughter would say, to realize they indeed have the potential existing inside of them to change their lives.

Be sure to make the time (a major priority if you are serious and committed to changing your life) to reflect on the potential lying dormant inside of you. What you have been conditioned to think becomes a part of the energy you emanate daily through your thoughts and language. This is your modus of operation. It's vital to ask yourself how you will get something different than what you allow your mind-set to constantly tell you.

This is a *huge* epiphany. I hope and pray you are able to recognize the self-empowerment you can bring into your life by recognizing this and doing something every day to develop and condition your mind-set for success.

Most people get stuck in their "comfort rut" and as a result do not realize their potential or ever begin to take action to change their lives. They are not even aware they can take charge and get something different than what they've been getting, that they truly have the potential to commit to do what it takes to get out of their rut.

If you are completely fed up with the immense pain in your life, then commit to using it as an inspiration, a springboard of motivation, to look within yourself to see your presently unrealized potential. Focus on your inspiration and exactly what it is you want in the form of your ultimate destination. Determine that the only option is to do what it takes. Figure out how to design a plan and the specific actions will get you there. Most importantly, you must begin. You have to take the first step to transform yourself and your life. Think about it as though you are an infant learning to walk. There is no giving up. You will keep getting up, and you will continually get better... and stronger... and more confident and more courageous.

Make a list of the specific aspects of pain you do *not* want in your life. That's right, make a list of the things you don't want in your life. Do not stop writing until you cannot think of anything else to add. This includes material things, situations, types of people, characteristics about yourself, even your relationships. Disappointment, being in debt, not making money...there is nothing that does not qualify for this list.

Take a break. Ten minutes at least. Now start a second list.

For every single item on the first list, write exactly the opposite, specifically *what it is you do want* for your life. This is an eye-opening experience. It's often easier to figure out what you don't want in order to open your eyes, mind and heart than figuring out what you do want.

Use this exercise to begin your new mode of self-empowering thinking.

- What type of person do you want to be?

- What values and characteristics do you want to have?

- What type of people do you want to have in your life? I would hope empowering people. No dream stealers or naysayers allowed. Period!

Next, go back through this list one item at a time and write down exactly what type of person you have to be in order to truly have that particular characteristic. You must be that person to attract what you want. If you're unfulfilled, it's because of the person you are being. If you don't do the work to strive toward becoming that person, nothing will change. It's really important for you to understand this.

If you haven't done so yet, sit down and write your list! Do it now. Otherwise use the voice recorder on your cell phone to record your initial list of what you don't want, and then the list of what you do want. Be creative and take initiative. There's always a way! When you return to your home or office, play this list back and write it down. This part is very important as it makes the exercise real. As Tony Robbins teaches, "Never leave the site of setting a goal without at least taking some form of action. Never!"

Visualizing exactly what you want is a proven, effective way to nurture and establish a self-empowering mind-set. There are various ways to visualize your ultimate destination. Two methods have been extremely effective for me.

One of these is the "energy circle." This concept comes from *Know How to Be Rich* by Dr. Robert Anthony. The energy circle involves making a list of "I am" statements stating the type of person you want to be, the strengths you want to have and what you want in your life. Speak these statements as though you are that person now. The list includes things, such as values, characteristics, and strengths. Examples are "I am rich; I am wealthy; I am loving; I am loved; I am grateful for who I am; and I am grateful for who I am becoming." The possibilities are endless and needs to include any characteristic or skill-set that empowers you to achieve your goals.

Take your "I am" list and draw an imaginary circle on the floor. Speak your statements with heartfelt conviction into the circle. When you are done, step into the circle and embrace the spoken statements. Take the energy of this moment and truly embrace this mind-set of "I am" completely.

Seem silly to you? That's okay. What you are really doing is creating a daily ritual to develop your new self-empowering mind-set. It works, so what do you have to lose? The catch is you must do it with conviction and absolute belief of your "I am" statements.

Visualize where you want to be as though you are already there. Get it? Great!

It's time to share a few things to open your eyes, to help you understand and believe you already have this incredible gift of potential waiting to be unwrapped. (This is a great visualization. Picture yourself ripping open a present. The wrapping paper symbolizes stripping away your fears so you can get to your inner potential, one of the most amazing gifts you can ever give yourself.)

Everyone, including you, has excelled at something. Think about what these experiences, these talents, these accomplishments, look like for you.

- Are you good at sewing?

- Do you have athletic talents you've spent hours practicing and honing?

- How about singing?

- Do you play a musical instrument?

- Are there certain games you almost always win?

- Do you like to fish?

- Are you an amazing storyteller?

- Do you clean like nobody else you know?

- Do you love art and have the talented gift of drawing, painting or sculpting?

- What other creative talents do you have?

- Maybe you're really good with animals. (There's a truly inspiring story about a young Mexican, Cesar Milan, who loved dogs and became "The Dog Whisperer." His passion became his extraordinarily successful reality.)

There is something you're good at, at least one major accomplishment you've had in the past. Think about this and take the time to write it down in detail. And remember that success is absolutely in the eyes of the beholder. By recognizing you've been successful at something, you can take this real-life experience and use it to build on the success you dream about now. Success means different things for everyone, and it's not about the money. The money is a side effect of your passion. It's about what you can do with the money and this is what you must focus on, what it is you really want. It's important to realize that money is simply the vehicle. It is not the end goal.

From as early as I can remember, I loved playing sports, particularly baseball, soccer, football, and tennis. I played three sports in high school and two sports my first two years of college.

Though I was fast and coordinated, I wasn't automatically good at any of these sports the first time out. I had to practice to develop the skills. So, practice I did, constantly.

During my sophomore and junior years of college, I subconsciously let my fear of not being good enough and being afraid to go talk to my coaches steal my passionate dreams of sports. My freshman year of college, I made both the varsity soccer and baseball teams. Yet, for some reason I was afraid to talk to the baseball coach. I'd only played in one game my freshman year and went one for two. Insignificant? Maybe, but it was pretty big to me. My subconscious fears kept me from going back for tryouts my sophomore year.

I was starting on the varsity soccer team my sophomore year, until I got sick with ten-day measles. I worked hard afterwards, but the coach didn't start me again that season. My fear said it was okay for me to use this as an excuse, and I did not go back to the team my junior year.

Still wondering what the good news is from these choices and if there's an epiphany? In hindsight, I completely realize that subconsciously I allowed my fears to steal my dreams of playing two varsity sports for four years in college. I initially felt pretty stupid about this, until I realized the value of the lessons I've learned about fear and how they can steal your dreams if you let them. Hindsight can be painful at times, but the lessons are invaluable when you have gratitude.

I now know I will *not* allow my fears to steal my dreams ever again. I am resolved and I am committed. My prior sports experiences opened my eyes to the tremendous potential within me. I made the varsity teams! I met this challenge that many do not ever achieve. From this point forward, I will *not* ever quit! After all, quitters never win.

If you are resolved and resolutely committed, then know you can absolutely tap into your potential. This is the first step to you being well on your personal journey to your success. (Do be aware that having a large ego does *not* apply here).

Another eye-opening epiphany I had was when I realized that my personal journey to the success I visualize daily was not about finding a specific business. I used to think that if I found the right business opportunity and focused on it, my life would change. *Not so.*

This additional life-transforming epiphany arose from my repeated frustration of finding a business at the time I thought was the answer, then another…and yet another. I was still getting nowhere.

Then the electrifying, shocking, eye-opening epiphany hit me. I had been focusing on the wrong thing! I was focused on making money, not on my purpose or passion. I realized I had to work on myself if I was to tap into my own incredible potential. I had to figure out what I wanted, come up with a plan of action and focus on the action taking process to get me there.

I became aware of what I had to do for my dreams to become my reality. I had to read, study, and learn to develop the competence necessary for success and then apply myself and what

I'd learned and take *action*. I had to get out of my comfort rut and start doing things I was initially uncomfortable with. Why? Because this is what leads to personal transformation and growth, to true self-refinement. This is what success is all about. You must become the person, the leader it takes to get to where you want to be and to have the success you really want! Think about this.

You can't be a world-famous chef if you don't know how to cook incredibly wonderful food. You can't become a world-class ballerina without practicing daily. There's no way you can become a respected, world-renown economist if you aren't an expert in economics. Do you think you can become an envied race-car mechanic if you don't know everything about engines and racing? You have to learn and practice by breaking down engines and rebuilding them, over and over again and spend time with world-class mechanics to learn firsthand. (This can also serve as networking as you begin to build your own reputation.)

Do you think Richard Branson, Donald Trump, or Boone T. Pickens don't continually work on themselves? The greatest leaders, no matter how successful they are, continue to learn something new, so they can expand their knowledge and skills to refine and fulfill yet another aspect of their amazing potential.

Upon reaching the next level of success or achieving the next goal, your aspirations and goals will transform to yet something else. There is always something new to learn, a new epiphany lurking around each and every corner of life.

Your potential is limitless. Let this be a major epiphany for you. Tapping into your potential is only up to one person— yep, the person you see in the mirror every morning. The Michael Jackson song, "Man in the Mirror," sums this up. Start with small steps every day. Progress does not come after a single action. It takes commitment, focus, inspiration, a plan, consistent daily action, and patience.

So, where and how do you begin to recognize you have potential inside of you and what do you do to start to tap into it? Stay tuned for an inspirational story...

CHAPTER EIGHT

COURAGE PRINCIPLE 3:
UNREALIZED POTENTIAL CONT.
FORGING YOUR NEW MIND-SET: FORMING NEW HABITS, ROUTINES, AND RITUALS

Give me six hours to chop down a tree
and I will spend the first four sharpening the ax.
– Abraham Lincoln

Write down your goals to make them real!

To begin to realize your potential, you must change your beliefs, know what you want, and take action. You will transform yourself and change your life!

Recently, I heard an amazing young woman tell her story at a monthly meeting for a mentoring program for teenagers from East St. Louis, Illinois. This determined young woman broke the stereotypical mold of her environment. Against the odds of being stuck deeply in a poverty mind-set and being deeply conditioned by her culture, she now has a college degree, a good job, a car, and owns and manages multiple properties.

Now this may not seem like a big deal to you, but when you find out she is one of only 4 out of 64 people in her entire family with a car, that may wake you up. At age 18, she realized she knew what she absolutely did not want. She also somehow knew she had the potential to change her life. How did she do it?

Tracey Wayne is now an inspirational 27 year old. She is a living, breathing example of what is possible when you recognize your inner potential. After hearing Tracey speak at the Join Hands meeting for mentors and their mentees, where we are both mentors, I was so inspired I had to introduce myself and get to know her. Her story is one that demonstrates you can indeed commit to changing your life and doing what it takes to beat the odds.

East St. Louis is one of the most impoverished cities in the United States. The school system there is not known for its quality education. The environmental combination of home life and the local school system does not lend itself to empower kids to realize they have incredible potential within themselves for their success.

Imagine being told over and over again that you can't do things because you can't afford it or simply being told no constantly.

This sounds more like an incubator for creating an impoverished mind-set, one holding you back for the rest of your life, unless you get sick of the pain of being stuck and commit to doing what it takes to move forward.

This is exactly what drove Tracey to creating a different path for herself. When she was 18, she decided she was sick of the pain of being poor. Tracey made a resolute commitment to do whatever it would take to get a college degree so she could get a decent job and start to live life on her own terms, *not* in poverty, the way everyone else assumed she would live it.

Tracey's back was up against the wall. She couldn't take it anymore, and she committed to doing something about it. She knew failure was not an option. She had to succeed. She laid out a plan and started taking focused action.

Fortunately for Tracey, she had two aunts who were able to take her places. Even this little bit of travel opened her eyes to the possibilities the world had to offer. She saw and experienced things she had never seen or dreamed of. It was an awakening of sorts for her as she realized she had no idea what she didn't know. She wanted to find out more about what she didn't know, and she knew she had the potential within herself to start finding out more.

There were still struggles and challenges during her college years. For a while, she surrounded herself with friends who were not focused on school or their futures. They were more into hanging out and partying. As a result, by her junior year, her grades suffered. Guilt started to take over. She realized how important her environment was. Though it was hard, especially at first, she let go of the individuals emanating a negative influence and began building a new core group of more empowering and positively influential friends.

Tracey spent a semester abroad in Paris, which really opened her eyes to the immense possibilities the world holds when you start to realize your potential. She applied herself her senior year and ended up getting a solid job in accounting across the river in St. Louis, Missouri. She is a now a landlord and owns several rental properties.

Tracey says her biggest challenge was with her father, who left when she was young and remarried. She was not allowed to speak with her sisters from her dad's second marriage. He never called her. She was afraid to reach out to them. She finally became fed up with this pain and reached out to her sisters. They are now developing relationships and becoming good friends. Though she was afraid her father would further distance himself, Tracey has been pleasantly surprised that her dad now calls her and even visits at times.

Tracey took personal responsibility, decided what she wanted, and went after it. Tracey refused to be a victim of her circumstances. Everything is working out as a result. She is committed to not letting her fears take over ever again.

She is taking action, learning, refining herself, and blossoming into an incredibly inspired and ambitious young woman, who also happens to give back to those less fortunate. Tracey has worked on herself and now has a self-empowering mind-set. She has formed new habits and routines. As a result, she has changed her life. She has broken the constrictive mold of her prior environment and entered the realm of the 4 percent of those who do what it takes so they can live their life by their own design.

Every single one of us is where we are in life because of the person in the mirror. Likewise, every one of us can get to where we really want to be because of that same individual. It's up to you to figure out where you are, what you want, and what you need to do to get there. You are both the cause of where you are and the solution for being able to get to where you want to be.

If you absolutely love where you are, what you have, and who you are, then I am ecstatic for you and know you must be truly happy and fulfilled. I'm sure you have worked diligently in your ongoing journey of self-refinement. You probably find yourself smiling every time you look in that morning mirror! You are one of the rare breed who is committed to always work on yourself, to consistently improve your mind-set and skill set. Major kudos to you for not being complacent, for this is when things start to spiral downward.

Then again, if you're miserable and completely fed up with what you're getting in life right now, get your highlighter out, grab a glass of water, do 20 jumping jacks to get the blood flowing…take a few slow, deep breaths, get excited, and commit to start forging ahead!

If you're at all like me, you always want something more in your life, for your family, for yourself, and you dream about being able to live life the way you really want. It's also likely that you are passionate about being able to positively impact the world.

My ultimate destination goes beyond materialistic things, though I really, really do want an Aston Martin Vanquish!

Know this... The day I place my hands on the steering wheel of *my* Aston Martin, push the start button and hear that smooth, powerful roar as the magnificent engine leaps to life, it will be definitively symbolic that I am getting close to realizing my potential. It means I will have impacted people's lives by inspiring and awakening them to find their own inspiration, to find their passion, their purpose. They will have started taking *action* in their own lives to transform themselves and change their lives.

An Aston Martin is about the experience, how you feel when you drive one. The day I sit in the plush, handcrafted leather seat of *my* Aston Martin, I will not only feel the glove-like fit of the seat caressing my body, I will feel the contribution I have started to make by inspiring individuals to realize they have their own incredible potential waiting to be tapped. It will be an incredibly fulfilling experience and the ride of my lifetime will have just begun! This is what an Aston Martin symbolizes to me.

From a materialistic standpoint, I have a question for you. Have you ever driven a super high-end sports car? Then you do *not* know what you are missing. Herein is a key point to life. You don't know what you don't know. So get out there and learn about the possibilities the world has to offer. Open your eyes, your mind, and your heart to what your passion may be and what the future can hold for you. Knowledge comes in many forms. Get curious and figure out what type of knowledge fills you with passion and get determined to do what it takes so you can actually experience the world in ways that will further fuel your passion. Knowledge by itself is, well it's just that, knowledge. Knowledge combined with *action* is empowering and life transforming.

When most people buy a car, they want transportation. Some "rides" are smoother, faster, better in snow, great for off-roading, get better mileage and so on, than others.

A truly high-end sports car is about the exhilarating experience. When I test drove the Aston Martin DB-9, considered the iconic symbol of Aston Martin by many, the passenger was my daughter, who at the time was twelve years old. At the end of the test-drive she exclaimed, "Dad, that was AWESOME!"

Two years later I test-drove a DBS. This took "unbelievable" to an entirely new level of experience! I want to earn that *awesome* experience of driving my own life, which for me is symbolized by this amazing car!

Does this make sense? If not, that's okay. Do realize however, that you don't know what you don't know. Think about this and make the choice to open your eyes, mind and heart to the possibilities of the world. Commit to figure out which of these possibilities you want in your life.

If you don't know what you want, how can you possibly know what actions you need to take each day? If you don't know what inspires you, how can you be motivated to take consistent and inspired action? If you don't know what a specific experience feels like, what emotions you feel, then how can you really be emotionally driven to have the experience?

If you think there is something you really want, yet you've never actually experienced it, then get out there and expose yourself to it. At least learn about it. Books in any form, are not only a way of learning, they can open your imagination to new realms of possibility.

This could mean reading about a special place in the world, which you then set as a specific goal so you can experience it firsthand.

If watching a movie and seeing a destination for the first time really gets you excited or curious, then find pictures to make a dream board, movie, or slide show, and set it to music so you can watch it first thing every day. This is a wonderful way to visualize your dreams and get your mind-set in the best possible place to start your day. Visualization of what you want is key.

Every morning there are several mind-set rituals I go through. I love watching my morning slide show, which I set to various energizing, adrenaline-pumping music. When the four to five minute show is done, I am super psyched to take action to make progress toward my ultimate destination. I spend a few minutes speaking "I am" statements, summing up the person I am becoming, my values, my talents, and so on.

These two rituals take less than 10 minutes and get me in an amazing frame of mind. I am excited, energized, and focused on what I want, and I get to work. I am conditioning my mind-set to be in the place where I already have the things I want and the mind-set for whom I want to be as though I already am that person, that leader.

You are where you are because of the habits that have been conditioned throughout your life. Many, if not most, of these are subconscious. In large part, because of your environment and culture, the resulting conditioning may have led to a negative mind-set that encumbers you and holds you back.

There is an eye-opening game that I was exposed to at a recent marketing event in Dallas, Texas. The speaker was an inspirational gentleman of purpose named Jim Bunch. As soon as Jim walked on stage I connected with his extremely high, charismatic energy. I immediately noticed he was carrying a glass fish bowl.

He told the audience that we would be playing the "Blame, Shame, Justify" game for the rest of the day. Any time an individual in the room realized they were blaming themselves or someone else, shaming themselves or someone else, justifying their actions, making an excuse for themselves or someone else, they owed two dollars to the fish bowl. The game required self-awareness, honesty, and integrity. That was it. These were the rules, the guidelines. The game started.

A woman went up to the stage almost immediately and placed two dollars in the glass fish bowl. Jim Bunch commended her for her integrity and continued with his inspirational and insightful presentation.

I found myself coming up with excuses for why my business wasn't doing better... I had too much going on... My mental red light started flashing, and I realized I owed two bucks! A few minutes later, I was heading back to the stage with two spots for the kitty as I had caught myself saying to myself, "Why is it I never follow through?" Then yet again for thinking how someone else had not done what they said they were going to do, in other words shaming them.

I soon ran out of single dollar bills. The next stage-bound visit I found myself depositing a 20-dollar bill. Jim had a funny look on his face as he was standing right in front of me. I said, "I'm simply paying in advance."

Next a cohort and friend walked to the stage and rather loudly stated, "I'm just paying for Peter," and laughter rippled through the audience. His wife hollered out that he had shamed me and owed two more dollars. She was right. What she didn't realize was that she had just shamed her husband and she owed two dollars! I realized if I pointed this out, I would owe two more dollars as I would be shaming her. The epiphanies from the lessons of the game had already started for me.

Herein was a huge revelation for how negatively conditioned my own mind-set was. Right then and there, I knew I had to transform and recondition my mind-set. It was mandatory to condition new thought processes, language, habits, daily rituals, and routines that would lead me directly toward success rather than keep me from it.

To this day, I have a glass cylinder on my desk I use to play the "Blame, Shame, Justify" game as a reminder of my mind-set. I play it with one dollar owed per instance of mind-set infraction. It is a travel kitty jar so to speak, trip destination to be determined.

I really hope this is more than just making sense to you. Perhaps you will realize how you have been negatively conditioned. Be totally honest and play this game yourself. The challenge for you is to see how the self-awareness of your mind-set is suddenly much more acute.

Having this initial awareness of whether your current mind-set is empowering you or holding you back is key to being able to change it, to condition it into the potentially empowering vehicle it was designed to be to take you to your ultimate destination. It's time to absolutely and resolutely commit to *stop* reacting to people and situations, to once and for all get rid of this self-defeating mind-set. It's time to fuel up, kick-start, and condition your new mind-set of self-belief and confidence.

Everyone has had success in some form or fashion. Use this knowledge as a stepping-stone to nurture your mind-set of belief to get you out of your comfort rut. Spend some time thinking about the things you have excelled at during your life. It doesn't matter if it was during childhood, your teenage years, or beyond. Because you've been able to develop a skill set once, you can absolutely do it again in a new area.

Here's an empowering exercise to help you tune into your strengths and become aware of your weaknesses. Simply follow these steps:

1. Write a list of your personal strengths until you cannot think of any more.

2. Prioritize your strengths and write down the top five in order on a separate list.

3. Write down what you think your weaknesses are, until you can't think of any more. This list is simply for you to be sure you're truly focusing on your strengths.

4. Now ask the three individuals who know you the best, the most intimately, to write down all of your strengths and to prioritize the top five. Do *not* tell them what is on your list.

5. Get these three lists and compare them to your own list of personal strengths.

6. Two to four items are going to be similar, the rest pretty different. That is a great thing! Your friends and family will be much more objective about you and your strengths.

7. Pay attention to the strengths on the three lists that are both similar to and different from the ones on your list. The ones that are different are your strengths as others see them. These will be very empowering for you as you learn how to focus on them and create strategic approaches.

8. Once you aware of your strengths and weaknesses, you definitely want to set goals that match up to your strengths and take specific actions to achieve them.

It's vital to stop reacting so you can start taking *proactive* action toward your goals. The next step is to develop and condition new habits to help you be laser focused and disciplined. Designing a systematized structure to help you get organized is essential for true productivity. How you use your time is ultimately key to minimizing distractions and being efficient.

Following your new systematized structure takes discipline. Make sure during your scheduled times of focused productivity, you do not allow any distractions. This means no cell phone calls, no e-mails, and *no* text messages! (Breaking these technological addictions may take some true awareness to stop reacting to every sound and vibration.)

You may be wondering what it means to set up a systematized structure. Begin with your destination and figure out the last action step you will take to get there. Now continue working backwards until you get to the starting point, where you are now.

Set aside specific time each day with strict guidelines where *nothing* will distract you or keep you from being *productive*. Communicate your expectations to those in your physical environment, such as family members, friends, or coworkers that during the specific time you set, you cannot be interrupted for anything other than a true emergency, no exceptions.

There are productivity and accountability systems out there to help you prioritize your actions and use your time efficiently and productively. One of the best is Might Club, which was designed by Patrick Combs and Mike Budny. Might Club has been a tremendous asset for me. It helped me develop laser focus, discipline, and accountability. Might Club has a built-in system with live coaches to help keep you on track and stay motivated.

One of the biggest lessons I've learned from Might Time is to really empower myself for productivity, to cut down on the seemingly endless to-do lists and write down the three highest priorities for the next day, actions that will directly lead to achieving my goals and get me closer to my destination. To check out MIGHT Club, simply go to http://mightclub.org/the-might-system/

Important note: Being productive is completely different from being busy. Make sure your actions will directly lead to accomplishing your goals. This will ensure that you are really being productive. Make sure to know the distinction.

Got it? Über awesome!

In order to be successful, you must know what success means to you. You must develop and hone a mind-set of success in order to be successful. What does this mean? It means you must have the belief, the thought processes, and speak the language of success now, in the present. You must consistently *be* that person in the present.

So figure out exactly what you want, where you want to be and who, the type of person or leader you want to be and start learning the skill-sets it will take for you to become this unique, talented individual. You have the potential inside of you. To realize this potential, you *must* take *action*!

If you want to be a professional inspirational speaker, it's vital you learn about inspiration, beginning with what inspires you. You must put yourself out there, take action by getting in front of people, and speak in order to expand your comfort zone and build your confidence and communication skills while on your feet. Before actually getting in front of people, it would serve you well if you prepared yourself for what you were going to talk about and how you intend to share you message.

If your goal is to be a great litigator, you must not only know the law, you will need to observe the best and learn to do what they do. You must put yourself in litigating situations where you are on the front line.

Whatever it is you really want to do, the best way to begin is to take the first action step. That's generally one of the hardest obstacles to overcome. Every inspirational and successful individual has prepared to have courage when it comes to their craft.

There are three aspects of self-empowered learning that have made all the difference in the world for me.

- The best way to set an example is to live it yourself. It's also one of the most direct ways to inspire others.

- The most effective way to learn is to teach others. So teach others what you learn and you will solidify it into your core, into your mind-set.

- To take care of others, you must first take excellent care of yourself. Many people simply do not get this one and they are completely absorbed in giving everything they have to help take care of others and they end up being completely out of balance, having nothing left in their tank to give.

Without awareness of how important it is to take care of *you*, there may come a day when you feel completely drained, exhausted, and fed up. You may feel you are incapable of doing anything for anyone else because you'll be filled with resentment. So take care of yourself by taking a little "you" time each day—fitness, nutrition, quiet time, reading, walking, meditating—whatever it is that brings you balance.

Set aside a specific time each day for 30 to 90 minutes to have your own, as Tony Robbins would say, Personal Power Hour. Take five minutes to visualize your destination, speak powerful "I am" statements. Take care of your body by working out or walking. Get some form of exercise. Make this a daily ritual.

Figure out what time of day your energy is highest, and use this time to focus on your main priorities, the actions that will move you closer to your goals. Be disciplined, be consistent, and be patient. Keep your eyes on the prize!

Focusing on the money will not bring you the money. When you figure out the specific actions you need to take to make progress toward your goals and your destination, focus on the process, what it is that you must do to be diligent in consistently taking these actions. By focusing your strengths and energy on the process, you will be empowering yourself and things will begin to happen. The key is that in order to achieve monetary goals, it's essential to focus on the process it takes to get to the goals, not on the money.

This will change how you look at things and how you approach goal-setting and challenges. You will take actions with confidence, choose to take personal responsibility, and always follow through. You will do what it takes to get your daily goals accomplished. When you're consumed with self-doubt (which comes from fear), you'll end up feeling overwhelmed. You'll procrastinate and never take the actions necessary for your success.

A life-changing aspect of conditioning new habits, rituals, and routines that is often overlooked is your environment. The impact that your environment has on you was introduced to me by Jim Bunch. Initially, I thought he was strictly speaking about the physical environment around you, such as your home, your office, or wherever it is you get your work done.

Your physical environment is a key component. It's amazing how the energy of a space changes, for example, when you rearrange furniture or paint your living room or home office. The energy in your work space is really important.

Getting rid of the clutter is a key part of your environment. Clutter is distracting. When you're working on transforming yourself or building your business, you want to be disciplined and focused, so no more clutter. Take a few days and clean it up. File it. Trash it. Get it neat and organized, so you can start being more productive than ever before.

Maybe the most influential aspect of your environment is the people in your life, particularly those you spend the most time with. They will have the greatest impact on you. The energy you put out there via the person you are and are becoming attracts like-minded, energetic individuals. Take a few deep breaths. It's time to ask yourself some very direct questions about the people you surround yourself with.

- Is their mind-set conducive to your success?

- Are they empowering you or disempowering you for success?

- Are they honest and direct when they say they are concerned about you?

- Is their mind-set actually negative and their advice conflicting with your goals and draining your energy?

- Are they telling you that you'll never be able to be successful at what you're doing?

If this is the reality, then these people are dream-stealers, they are the naysayers in your life. If you are serious and committed about transforming yourself and changing your life, about realizing your goals and dreams, then it's time to put some distance between yourself and these toxic individuals.

Even if you have known someone most of your life, if they are not empowering you, you can at least choose to limit the time you spend around them and how you interact with them. It is important to communicate your boundaries to the people in your life in a constructive way. Once you've done this, if someone continues to cross the boundaries you've set, it's time to bid *adieu*, to say *adios*.

How serious and committed are you? Respect is important and it needs to be mutual. If it's not, it's time to move on, to find empowering people you can add into the inner most circle of your life. Moving on to tap into your unrealized potential, you must take personal responsibility for your choices.

CHAPTER NINE

COURAGE PRINCIPLE 4: RESPONSIBILITY

*You have to do your own growing
no matter how tall your grandfather was.*
– Abraham Lincoln

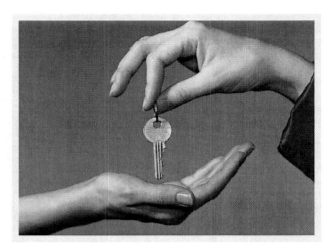

How many people do you know who always blame their circumstances on someone or something else? Do you know anyone who seems to always think they're a victim of their circumstances? These individuals have no clue whatsoever about the concept of consistently taking personal responsibility. The bottom-line reality is it's a result of their own choices that have led them directly to where they are now. There is limitless empowerment in coming to terms with this self-realization, which begins with personal responsibility.

Just what does it mean to have and take personal responsibility? Responsibility is all about integrity. Integrity begins within you. When you say you are going to do something, taking responsibility means following through and doing it when you say you'll do it. This is just as important when you promise yourself as it is when you tell someone else you will take a specific action. This is essential in order to have and maintain integrity.

There will be times when something slips through the cracks. It's possible there is a solid reason or even an emergency that kept you from being able to follow through. It could even be you simply forgot to look at your schedule and missed a meeting. Or you simply didn't feel like doing something you either promised yourself or someone else you'd do. (By the way, taking full personal responsibility means you will still follow through when you don't feel like it.)

So how do you return to a place of integrity if you've gotten out of sync with integrity? First, you must take ownership for being out of a place of integrity. In coaching, the term *out of integrity* is often used to describe this behavior. It is not someone else's fault. It is not because something else happened. Admit your mistake to yourself and to anyone else who is impacted. Apologize for having lost integrity. Commit to taking the next step to return to complete integrity.

Learn and grow from your mistakes. When you have lost integrity with someone else, you're out of integrity with yourself. Know that when you consistently lose integrity, you are going the opposite direction you want to go. You are not heading toward your ultimate destination. You are not accomplishing your goals. You will not be attracting leaders into your life. You will be deterring true leaders from entering your inner circle.

Always be honest with yourself. Do not make up excuses. Excuses are lame. So, when you tell someone you will call them at a certain time, do what it takes to make sure you call them. Set an alarm on your cell phone. Put a sticky note on your computer. Condition yourself to always follow through. If you don't or can't, then it's vital to pick up the phone and apologize in a straightforward fashion and reschedule.

Before his passing, I remember asking a lifetime friend of my mother's the following question: "Sid, with the success you've had and all of your life experiences, if you could give me just one piece of advice, what would it be?" Without hesitation, Sid replied, "To always follow through on what you say you'll do." This is the definition of taking personal responsibility.

Though I did not know him very long, I considered Sid to be a very down to earth, wise, and truly successful man. Sid had been an expert in the specialized field of international communications for the airline industry. He had traveled the world, met many amazing people, and seen so much in his 90-plus years.

After much reflection and journaling, I realized the advice Sid shared with me was spot on. One will not be successful without having consistent follow through. Follow through equates to integrity, which is what taking personal responsibility is all about. To become a leader, you must follow through. Sid, I thank you from the bottom of my heart. I miss you and I miss our conversations.

Responsibility is key as you embark on your committed journey to success. If you feel stuck in the comfort rut that's become your life and you really want to climb out, you must know where you are now, figure out where you want to be, and come up with your plan of action in order to gain the traction needed to climb out of that rut. You must follow through by taking action to generate momentum, so you can transform yourself and change your life.

A future epiphany for you is that as you begin to condition your self-empowering mind-set and the more consistently you take action, the more inspired you will feel and the more progress you will make. You will also begin to attract more like-minded people into your life.

Focus and discipline must become a part of your daily routine. This includes making sure you do not allow any distractions during your true productivity time. No e-mails, no answering your phone, no sending texts, no Facebook time. Concentration for pure focus on the action you are taking, on the process at hand, is key. Minimizing frustration and having patience are important ingredients to your recipe for progress. Being consistent in such a manner, you will be amazed at what will begin to happen, what you will attract into your life, the type of people who will start to enter your life and the progress toward success you will start to achieve.

Taking personal responsibility and holding yourself accountable is a prerequisite for true progress and for your success. This means your goals need to be measurable and trackable. You must be able to track your performance so you can determine if you are getting closer to your goals or farther away. It's okay to occasionally move farther away from your goals. With the proper mind-set, you will realize this is not failure, rather it's about learning what doesn't work, so you can adjust your actions and refocus to get back on the path you want to be on. If you don't track your performance, how will you know when you've gotten off track or if you're getting closer to achieving your goals?

An excellent principle for true enlightenment and transformation is to not take anything personally. This can be an extremely challenging lesson to understand and actually apply. The premise is that no matter what words come out of someone else's mouth, no matter what actions or inactions they take, what they are saying and what they are doing are a direct result of their own personal past conditioning and experiences and has absolutely nothing to do with you.

Think of it this way. When you can focus on what it is you want, when you are being the person that will attract exactly this via your own words and actions, you will not react to someone else's words or actions. Even if someone purposefully intends to emotionally hurt you or they get angry at something you've said or done, if you do not react to them, you will be much more likely to get what it is you want. It's a matter of being aware and conscious.

If someone else is reacting to their subconscious fears and lashes out at you, when you continue to remain calm and consciously aware, and can ask yourself what you need to say or do next so you can get what you want, you will still be in control of yourself and of the situation. Whenever someone is being reactive, it means they have lost control, of both their emotions and of the situation. When you react in return, you have also relinquished your own control. Wouldn't you rather remain in control so you are more likely to get what you want?

I really hope this makes sense to you. If you need more in-depth information on this principle, you may want to pick up a copy of *The Four Agreements* by Don Miguel Ruiz. This principle will transform your relationships and subsequently, your life.

Your success is up to you, so when you get to that place where you commit to achieving your goals, you must have integrity from that point forward in order to arrive at your destination. This means taking personal responsibility in all areas of your life.

The next principle is to develop a keen level of self-awareness so that your fears are not a "drag on" your true potential.

CHAPTER TEN

COURAGE PRINCIPLE 5: AWARENESS
AWARENESS OF WHAT IS HOLDING YOU BACK AND STOPPING THE VICIOUS CYCLE OF SUBCONSCIOUS FEAR

Every human has four endowments—self-awareness, conscience, independent will, and creative imagination. These give us the ultimate human freedom…The power to choose, to respond, to change.
– Stephen Covey

Subconscious fears are your dragons. They are a "drag on" your ultimate potential. Without awareness, your fears (your dragons) will always win, and you will be stuck in that proverbial rut. Having awareness of this is key to being able to overcome this obstacle so you can begin moving forward. How much time and thought have you spent reflecting on what is holding you back, keeping you from getting what you want? If you're ready to start a self-empowering revolution, here's some fuel for your fire.

Why is it that so many people do the one thing that will definitely keep them from being able to live the life they want, from being able to achieve their goals (assuming they actually set goals)? For the 2 to 4 percent that do what it takes, who have the vision, focus and discipline to get to their ultimate destination, this is unfathomable

If you are absolutely committed to transforming your life, quitting is not an option. One of my favorite sayings is, "If your life is full of challenges and problems, and life isn't what you want it to be, look in the mirror. There is the cause...and there is the solution!"

I have known this saying for a very long time and realized it is absolutely true. The sad irony for me personally is for a long time I did not take action on the solution. Until the past few years, I had not worked to develop the mind-set and skill-sets that would allow me to make progress to become the person I really wanted to be, that I had to be, in order to make progress toward my ultimate destination. I had spent a lot of time delving into the cause part of the equation. As a result, I know without any doubt what is the biggest obstacle to success for anyone.

It's subconscious fear.

It's important to be aware of your subconscious fear, but where does it come from?

Subconscious fear is deeply embedded. It has been molded in various ways your entire life, beginning with childhood. It is in a sense the culmination of the aftereffects of how your parents raised you. It's the combination of your choices you've made and your life and relationship experiences. My own personal experiences will help shed some light on the "vicious cycle of subconscious fear".

Beginning at a very young age, it seemed my father corrected almost everything I did. If it wasn't his way, it was wrong. I loved my father very much. However, we did not have a relationship based on open, two-way, below-the-surface, meaningful communications. It was pretty much one-sided.

Initially, I was unaware that over time I stopped trying to express my thoughts and feelings, first to my father and then to almost anyone else. One of the most vivid examples of an interaction with my father was when I was probably between eight and ten years old.

My mother was looking for some specific jewelry to wear. When we were young, my sister and I used to play a lot of "dress up" games and do impromptu plays and role-playing. My father, for some reason, insisted that I had been the last person to see the jewelry and kept demanding that I find it. Since I had no idea where it was, of course, I kept returning without the jewelry. Every time I came back without the "lost" jewelry, my father would whip me with a belt as punishment.

I never spoke about this traumatizing experience with my father. I do not know if he was punishing me because he thought

I was lying or if the jewelry ever turned up. I do know he was *not* listening to me. He must have been reacting to his own deeply embedded fears and was probably punishing me the way his own father, my grandfather, used to punish him.

I do remember being completely confused and very angry at my father. Honesty had always been promoted and encouraged in our family, and I was being punished for being honest. After this experience, whenever my father asked me a question, I gave him the shortest possible answer I could think of and would almost always tell him what I thought he wanted to hear.

Over time, I not only shut down and lost my ability to communicate in meaningful ways, but I lost touch with my very own thoughts and feelings. When asked a question, I would feel paralyzed and not know what I thought or felt and often not say anything at all. I completely shut down and would walk away, fuming with anger and frustration. This was a direct result of the self-consuming fear I had about being wrong…yet again!

In hindsight, I realize how stifling my own thoughts and actions were and how my father was conditioning me to react with subconscious fears that were being deeply embedded in me. At such a young age, I had no idea that it was actually up to me whether or not continue to react in such a fear-based mode.

This subconscious, fear-based reactiveness continued until much later in my life. With all of the work I've done, I am now able to have much more epiphany-filled reflections during my "moments of hindsight" when I think back to prior experiences and how I dealt with them. Gratitude will enlighten you to the opportunity existing in every situation in the next chapter.

In the past, my subconscious, fear-based reactions not only impacted me in relationships, it affected the individuals in those relationships. My behavior and my reactions were disempowering to me and to the other person. I have now consciously chosen to recognize my old ways and committed to moving forward with the new-and-improved version of me. I have committed to being my best self.

Before working diligently on developing a truly heightened sense of self-awareness, every time someone disagreed with me or told me I was wrong, it was as though my father was lurking in the background correcting me, telling me I was wrong once again. Without any awareness of what was going on deep inside my subconscious, I lost my self-confidence. For much of my life, it was a challenge to foster and nurture relationships, not just with the women I've been in relationships with but with family and friends as well.

Being where I am today, knowing what I know, I am grateful for the opportunity I've had to rise to the challenge of developing both an awareness of my fears and the awareness of what I want. They are complete diametric opposites. If you don't know what you want, it's impossible to make progress to break out of your comfort rut.

I have spent a lot of time studying , learning about and discussing the cause and effect aspects of fear with professionals and with my mentors. And of course, I've spent much time reflecting on fear and writing about it. Fear is without a doubt the single biggest obstacle to success for everyone.

You may have read books by such notable authors and inspirational experts as Tony Robbins, Stephen Covey, Darren Hardy, Zig Ziglar, Dale Carnegie, and others. The list is pretty big. If you haven't had the opportunity to read any of their works, now is a good time to start reading. Knowledge combined with action is empowering and life transforming. So, if you think you don't like to read, this is definitely a part of your mind-set to start to change immediately to begin to empower yourself.

I hope the concept of "what you focus on is what you get" is not new to you. If you're reacting to your fears, then your fears will most likely come true because you are subconsciously focusing on them, and this means your fears are in control—the "vicious cycle of subconscious fear".

Coming up with a unique way to catch yourself each time you feel one of your fears being triggered is a great way to recondition yourself. Learn to "stop, think, and act" instead of continuing to let your fears be in control. My first signal method was to envision a picture of a little red flag popping out of the top of my head when I felt even the slightest hint of anger or trepidation during interactions with my now ex-wife. Then I started to take this mental picture to other areas when my fear would begin to creep in, so I could catch it before it became a true drag on being my best self.

Today I have a simple two-word question I ask myself that immediately brings me back to a place of balance and self-empowerment. When I feel myself about to react to any type of fear, whether it is anger, hesitation, frustration, and so on, I ask myself, "What's next"? This is the signal that I need to make sure the next words I speak or the next action I take will get me closer to where I want to be. Simultaneously, it is one of the most calming and empowering things I have ever said to myself.

Some people think they are shy. I used to be one of these. How did I start plowing through this fear? My first job out of college was in the travel industry, taking highly successful individuals on world-class trips they had won based on their job performance. Obviously, this job involved constant interaction with people. Next, I took a Dale Carnegie speaking class. And on the list goes.

Maybe you are afraid to make phone calls to prospects or people you don't know. I used to be afraid to raise my hand in class because of the fear of being wrong! There's no better way to learn than to put yourself out there. Plus, the fear diminishes the more you take action, resulting in a tremendous spurt of self-confidence.

Perhaps you have a fear of getting hurt in a relationship, so you keep your distance. Think about this seriously. How can you ever develop a wonderful relationship if you don't put yourself out there? If you're not your best self, you'll never attract that ultimate soul mate. Vulnerability is a key component of being your best self, to being the person you need to be to achieve your goals and to being a leader.

A now retired NFL football player had a huge fear of the water as a result of some childhood experiences. This Hall of Famer signed up for a scuba diving class to get over his fear of water. That's right. He took his biggest fear head on, and he didn't even know how to swim! He took on his fears headfirst and conquered them.

If you're afraid of failure, will you ever do what it takes to really succeed? You'll likely never even take the first step. How many people do you know who are stuck in this rut?

There are some people who actually have a fear of success. These individuals won't do what it takes to succeed either. Their fear halts them right in their tracks. They are probably asking themselves, "What will I do if this works and I achieve my goals?" A rather strange fear, but one I can personally relate to. This type of fear will trap you in a constant whirlpool of procrastination, never going anywhere.

Fear comes in all shapes and sizes. Keys to overcoming fears are:

- Become aware of your fears.

- Know what you want.

- Focus exactly on what it is you do want.

- Focus on becoming the person you must be to achieve your goals.

- Take consistent action to make progress toward what it is you *do* want.

- **To develop courage, you must prepare yourself (the main premise of this book!).**

There is another major key to stopping the vicious cycle of subconscious fear. This epiphany came to me when my personal Success Coach, JT DeBolt asked, "Peter, what single value, when you're completely filled with it, leaves no room for fear?" I responded, "It must be love." JT said, "No. It's gratitude."

This revelation has changed how I look at things and has opened my eyes, my mind, and my heart. Gratitude has allowed me to find opportunity in every situation, including changing how I look at past experiences, which subsequently empowers me for what action I will take next. Gratitude is indeed a major key that will change your life.

When you're unaware you are focusing on and reacting to your fears, it is impossible to be your best self. As you develop an increased and acute level of awareness for when you are reacting to your fears, you can begin to learn what the triggers are to your fears. Maybe it's a person, such as a parent or spouse. Or maybe it's when your subconscious thinks you are being criticized (wow, how I can relate to this one).

Everyone has different types of fears. It's up to you to reflect on your fears and what's holding you back. Life is about the conscious choices you make. Choose to jump into the fire and figure out your fear triggers. This is the starting point to permanent transformation so you can change your life.

Have you ever felt like someone let you down when they did not meet your expectations? Did you communicate your expectations to that individual in advance? If not, then no wonder you were disappointed. Think about this. Write down your thoughts so you can figure out how to empower yourself regarding your expectations instead of disempowering yourself.

Have you ever jumped to an erroneous conclusion about something someone said or did? This is another result of fear.

Taking things personally, whether it's something someone said or did, is a direct fear-based reaction. Even if someone does something to spite you or with the intent of revenge for something you said or did to them (and here's the vital key), if you don't take it personally, your next actions (versus your reactions when your fears are in control) will be different and much more self-empowering.

When you don't take things personally, you are much more in control of what will happen next. This means you will be able to stay in control of your emotions and remain calm. By asking yourself, "What next?", you can choose the best action to take or the best thing to say, a well-thought-out nonreactive choice that will get you closer to where you want to be and to even defuse a heated situation.

You have most likely experienced frustration more than once when your angry reaction begets more anger from the person you're interacting with. It becomes an ongoing crescendo of one accusatory outburst after another. Both parties end up fuming and nothing positive has been accomplished. Can you relate to this?

Anger means you are out of control. Do you think you will get what you really want when you're yelling at someone? Even with your children, you are setting an example of anger which they are very likely to repeat throughout their lives. When you react in anger to something someone says or does, one of the most striking epiphanies you will ever have is to realize that it is *not* the other person who angers you. It's true. It's your fear that's causing you to react with such anger, not the other person.

When you are aware, you can consciously choose to remain calm and deal with any situation without anger. This means you are in control in the present moment and that by stopping, thinking and choosing proactive action, you are more in control of what will happen next.

You cannot change or control the other person. You can work on changing and controlling yourself. When you change your own behavior from a conditioned reactive state (conditioned within you and often as far as subconscious expectations for how you will react by the other person) to a consciously controlled, calm state, you are setting a different, much more beneficial and empowering example.

Over time, the other person will have to change their behavior in interactions with you in order to get what they want as what they were doing previously is no longer working.

From this point forward in your life, choose whether you want to set an example of remaining calm, being conscious and dealing with conflict in a consistently empowering manner…or to set the example of being a fear-based, reactionary, angry, and irrational maniac. So…which do you choose?

This is huge. If you're having difficulty grasping this concept of reality, be sure to spend some time here thinking, reflecting, and journaling. If you don't do the work, you won't experience the personal growth.

As discussed previously, fear leads to pain. When you reach the point where you are completely fed up with the pain in your life caused by your fears, it's time to get serious about making the conscious choice to not let fear run your life any longer. Spend time reflecting and figuring out what you do want, your ultimate destination. Focus on the process and actions to make progress toward what you do want, and use the pain to drive you toward fueling your desires to find the FIRE within, your purpose and passion, and choose to put forth the effort to transform yourself and change your life.

No matter how much we talk about fear, no matter how many times someone tries to get through to you, and no matter how much inspiration someone else attempts to give you, there is only one person who can help remove the obstacle of fear from your life. It's up to you and only you to apply what you've learned to take back control of your life, get to where you want to be, have what you want, and realize the amazing potential you have inside of you and to become the inspirational person you were meant to be.

A point of awareness that pertains to what you focus on is what you get, is resistance. Resistance means resisting whatever it is you don't want. When you are focused on resisting what you don't want, be aware that this will only bring you more of what you don't want, additional resistance. Resistance stems from fear, so again, do not focus on your fear. You must create what you do want. This begins with focusing on exactly what you want.

When you understand the "vicious cycle of subconscious fear" and recognize the importance of knowing and focusing on what you want, you will free yourself from the obstacles that have been holding you back. This will validate that you can indeed live life differently, with a laser focus on what it is you really want. Of course, there will be challenges along the path to your success. Being filled with gratitude will open up endless opportunities for you to learn, grow, and achieve your goals.

CHAPTER ELEVEN

COURAGE PRINCIPLE 6: GRATITUDE

*Gratitude unlocks the fullness of life.
It turns what we have into enough, and more.
It turns denial into acceptance, chaos to order,
confusion to clarity. It can turn a meal into a feast,
a house into a home, a stranger into a friend.*
– Melody Beattie

What single value when you're filled with it leaves no room for fear? Like me, you may think the answer is "love." It's not. The deeply revealing answer is "gratitude." When you are filled with gratitude, your entire outlook is altered to an extremely empowering state.

True gratitude allows you to see the opportunity in every situation, in every experience. This includes the past. Though you cannot literally change the past, having gratitude changes how you interpret the past, even in emotionally painful situations. When you are filled with gratitude, you are transformed. As a result, what you do in the future will be much more beneficial and empowering to you and everyone you are close to.

Before sharing how gratitude has transformed me and helped to change my life, here is a shocking story to enlighten you to the immense, life-altering power of gratitude.

On May 22, 2011, at 5:41 p.m., an EF-5 tornado touched down in Joplin, Missouri. En EF-5 is the category for the most powerful and dangerous of storms. In the case of this particular storm, there were several storm cells that actually merged, creating possibly the most devastating tornado in history.

Unlike most tornados, which blow through towns at speeds of up to 50 miles an hour, this storm crept slowly across Joplin for 32 minutes. The swath of the storm was three-quarters of a mile wide. It traveled through Joplin for six miles. Winds were measured up to 308 miles an hour.

The storm decimated everything in its path. Eight thousand structures, both residential and commercial, were crushed like cardboard boxes, lifted into the air, and completely destroyed. Some were simply gone. Four hundred businesses were annihilated with 1,150 people severely injured. One hundred sixty-two individuals lost their lives.

All of the 50,000 inhabitants of Joplin were impacted. Some people were hurt physically. A lot of people were impacted materialistically with the loss of their homes, cars, and personal belongings. I imagine that every inhabitant of Joplin was affected emotionally and psychologically.

Right now you might be thinking, how can gratitude have anything to do with this horrific story of devastation and loss of life?

Great question.

Recently, I attended a conference and heard an inspirational speaker talk about gratitude. Doug Hunt is from Joplin, Missouri. He shared his personal story of what turned out to be the day of May 22, 2011. One of Doug's hobbies is the weather. He knows how to read weather maps and charts, possibly as well as some meteorologists.

On the afternoon of May 22, Doug and his son were riding bikes. During a break, Doug checked the weather on his cell phone. Upon reading the weather map, he noticed two storm super cells that looked like they would soon be colliding. He knew trouble was brewing. Doug and his son immediately went to a friends house and took refuge in the basement storm shelter.

Within hours after the tornado had left its inconceivable wake of destruction and human carnage, people from surrounding states began showing up to help in any way they could. Initially, the main goal was to look for survivors buried underneath the crumbled splinters and piles of brick that remained of homes or places of work. Compassion obviously resonated from the hearts of every volunteer rescuer.

Doug shared how he had seen a line of over 300 ambulances from both familiar and unfamiliar cities and towns, all with their lights and sirens going. Gratitude radiated from Doug as he described the soul-piercing bass resonance caused by the uniquely immense and overwhelming sound.

It is a sound he wishes to never hear again.

The entire time we were driving the path of the storm, Doug shared story after story of survival and triumph. His eyes were teary as he spoke of the heroes who died protecting loved ones, of children miraculously discovered unharmed, of a woman looking into the oncoming storm and watching rooftops and even a petroleum tanker truck being lifted into the sky. There were seemingly endless astonishing stories of the many ways the tornado left its mark, eternally impacting the town and particularly the people of Joplin.

After making sure their families were safe, Doug and two close friends set out as a team to see how they could help the victims who had been in the direct path of the storm. The trio pulled up to an apartment complex which had been torn apart, the top floor and a half literally ripped off the buildings. They heard a woman screaming that her baby was missing. She had grabbed her young child and infant and taken refuge in a closet. When she awoke, her child was in her arms, and she shockingly realized her baby was gone.

Though also still in shock, when her apartment neighbors heard the woman screaming that her baby had been swept away by the storm, they also began searching. Minutes later, at least 70 yards away, someone saw a little foot sticking out of a piece of storm-rolled carpet lying on top of debris at what used to be a convenience store. They quickly and carefully unrolled the sodden carpet and found the baby, miraculously unscratched and unharmed. They returned the infant to the emotionally overcome and ultimately grateful mother.

Gratitude surely had to impact everyone involved in the search and everyone hearing the story, particularly when the baby was found unharmed. As Doug's eyes welled with heartfelt tears while telling this story, it was clearly evident he still felt the gratitude for the outcome of this particular story, forever embedded in his memory.

During the months following this historically monstrous storm, The New York Times, Time Magazine, and countless other media sources came to Joplin to see the devastation and hear firsthand a handful of the 60,000 plus individual stories. Apparently, one of the most surprising components of the overall story was that of the community of Joplin. There were hardly any instances of looting, which so often seems to be a side effect of natural disasters, particularly in larger cities. Rather, the people of Joplin came together with the assistance of many "outsiders" to clean, repair, and rebuild Joplin with passion, determination, and gratitude. This is a unique tribute to the people and to the entire city of Joplin. The biggest tribute of all was demonstrated by their true, heartfelt gratitude and how it empowered the entire community, a small town with a humongous, passionate *why*.

There are certainly people in Joplin who are still fearful every time the sky turns gray, who are filled with anger and stuck in a fear-based place of resentment as a result of the tornado that struck on May 22, 2011. Doug is not one of them. Rather, he is grateful that his family was okay. He is also grateful that thousands of people weren't killed by the tornado, being as dangerous and destructive a storm as it was. He is filled with gratitude for the thousands of people who came from seemingly all over the country to help the people of Joplin however they could. He is also grateful for the overwhelming emotional inspiration that drives him to share his message of passion and gratitude.

Doug's eyes continued to be teary as he spoke of more heroes who died protecting loved ones, of children miraculously discovered unharmed, of an elderly woman who was found several hundred yards from her home with only a broken arm and shared story after story of the seemingly endless devastation and emotional trauma. These were astonishing stories of the many ways the tornado left its mark, eternally impacting the town and particularly the people of Joplin.

I have immense gratitude for Doug Hunt, for what he went through, for the many ways he contributed to the community of Joplin, the example he has set for having gratitude even after enduring such a ghastly experience, and for sharing his experience, insights and emotions with me. Thank you, Doug. I am most grateful you have become a part of my inner circle.

Gratitude comes in many forms and can be different for everyone. The commonality is that it will add so much to your life if you consciously choose for it to become a part of your daily modus of operation. Bring gratitude inside of you and you will think a miracle has taken over your soul.

One month shy of our eight year "anniversary", the woman I thought would be my future wife, Kathy, came to me and said she couldn't take it any more. She said we had been arguing too much and that I always blamed this on her. She went on to express she felt I had been so self-absorbed in my own work, striving to get my life back to a place where I could do all the wonderful things I loved to do, that I had not had any awareness of her needs and had spent no time with her. She did not feel the connection she needed and she felt I had not made it a priority to nurture and grow our relationship.

Initially, I not only blamed all of these things on her, but I was relieved the relationship was over.

When gratitude truly entered my life a few months later, one of the first things I did was to write down a list of all the qualities and values I wanted in a lifetime soul-mate, that special person with whom I would spend the rest of my life.

Then I went back through the list item by item, thinking of Kathy. I was shocked to find every single item checked. I found myself feeling immense gratitude for how she had stuck by my side for so long, even though her needs were not being met and I had not made much effort to spend time with her because I was so self-focused. In spite of this, she had been there, by my side, supporting me and always willing to help in any way she could.

The impacting realization hit me very hard. I had completely messed up by being absolutely unaware and taking Kathy for granted. It was time for me to take ownership, personal responsibility. We met and I profusely apologized for the pain and agony my actions and inactions had caused her over the past few years. It was to be expected that she would not be in a place where she would readily jump back into a relationship with me unless she knew without any doubt I had really changed. She had heard my words before but had not seen the follow through. Doubt overruled and understandably so.

To this day when I reflect back with gratitude, I am most appreciative of Kathy, her values, her efforts, and even for the hardships we went through. Gratitude has allowed me to release any anger, frustration, and resentment and to learn from my prior inability to be aware and led to appreciation. Never again will there be an air of taking anything or anyone for granted in my life. Every day is a gift, and it is absolutely time I live it as such and demonstrate the gratitude I have for the most special people in my life. Thank you, Kathy, for you have forever impacted me and my life, in such an amazing and empowering way. I am filled with absolute gratitude for the truly wonderful times and experiences we shared. I am grateful for your love and for my love for you. I am eternally grateful for you and for the time we spent together. I hope your life brings you everything you desire.

It is impossible to change the past. It is powerful to alter how you look at the past and to be filled with gratitude for the opportunity to learn and grow for the future.

When my brother, Chris, died from ALS, it was devastating. He was also my best friend. The reality was nothing could change the fact he was gone. Anger, depression, frustration could have consumed anyone who knew this courageous and inspirational soul. Or, when reflecting back with gratitude on Chris and how he dramatically pursued his passions, first of music, then of finding ways to help individuals with neurological disorders, it would surely open your heart and soul to find a source of inspiration for yourself. If my brother could have such focus and put forth such effort in spite of the fact that he could not move or speak, then what excuse do you and I have to not pursue our dreams and live life with focused passion?

Chris lost his battle with ALS on February 16, 2005. Almost eight years later, his efforts are still impacting the world. He has truly left his mark on the world in the form of an incredible legacy. What do you want your legacy to be?

Gratitude will lead you to see and find the opportunity to learn from your past and to choose how to do things differently for your future.

So what is your choice going to be? To remain stuck, feeling frustrated and possibly angry? Or to bring heartfelt gratitude into your life, so you can tap into the opportunity that exists right now inside of you in the form of incredible potential?

Anger clouds and consumes. Gratitude opens your eyes and brings clarity and releases possibility and potential. Hesitation and procrastination preclude progress and the realization of your potential. Gratitude leads to finding the heretofore unrecognized lessons that lead to growth and empower you to look within yourself to recognize your potential. Self-doubt and disbelief stifle and lead you to being stuck in that proverbial rut. Gratitude leads to building self-confidence and believing in yourself so you can take empowered action to get out of that rut and create something new. Gratitude will indeed lead you to finding opportunity in every situation.

There are so many things in life for which to be filled with gratitude. Be grateful for your experiences and the challenges life brings and the lessons you will learn (particularly if you are looking for the lessons). Be grateful for the ability you have to be aware and commit to transforming yourself and changing your life as a result.

Be thankful for the special people in your life. Share how you feel about them. Let them know. Be grateful for your health, your ability to laugh, and for your life. Choose gratitude and experience firsthand its amazing empowerment. Living life with gratitude will help you to be your best self.

CHAPTER TWELVE

COURAGE PRINCIPLE 7: EXCELLENCE

*The will to win, the desire to succeed, the urge
to reach your full potential… these are the keys that
will unlock the door to personal excellence.*
– Confucius

When you apply the 7 Principles of COURAGE and strive
for excellence, to be your best self,, you truly have the key for
opening the doorway to your success.

Have you ever had the life-altering epiphany that the *choices* you make in the present moment will determine your *future*? This is a realization that every successful leader understands and applies to their life. It is an unknown anomaly for the majority of people who feel they are stuck and who blame their dire circumstances on anyone and anything other than the person in the proverbial mirror.

Ron Price wrote a book called *Treasure Inside: 23 Unexpected Principles That Activate Greatness*. He says that the single most impacting principle to transform your life is the one he calls *Choices*. Every choice you make has a consequence.

When you combine Ron Price's principle of choice with Tony Robbins' theory on pain and pleasure, it will really open your eyes and mind to how your actions, or inactions, either empowers or disempowers your potential. Every choice you make is based on either pain or pleasure. When you choose pleasure now, there is often pain later. On the other hand, when your initial choice is pain now, it will often lead to pleasure later. One almost always results in the other.

When you choose to work a few extra hours now, you will be able to spend time with your family or do something you love later. When you get home from work and head to the kitchen to grab a glass of wine or a beer and make a beeline to that irresistible couch to plunk down and watch TV, there is something you are not getting done that you'll have to deal with later. If you watch TV two hours a night, that's 14 hours a week you could be building your future. Are you having an "aha!" moment?

You gain knowledge through reading, taking classes, talking to people who are where you want to be in life. It is like finding the key to your success. This key is no good unless you take the action to pick it up, find the door that fits the key, put the key in the lock, turn it and walk through the doorway to your success. With knowledge plus action you have an empowering and momentum gaining combination, the solution. Of course, if you simply absorb random or meaningless knowledge, such as watching TV or heading out to the bars every night, you will never achieve your goals. If you don't take specific action that will get you closer to your goals, you will simply further entrench yourself where you are, or even head in the wrong direction.

There may be times when you take the time to design a self-empowering plan of action and find that a particular action has not served you well. This is why being able to track and measure the results and progress of your actions is key. When you realize an action is taking you farther away from your destination, you can take corrective measures and determine a new action to get you back on track.

Applying the 7 Principles of COURAGE requires your own version of Excellence to culminate in the ability to figure out your passion, to find the FIRE within you and to take consistent action. When you completely and resolutely commit to being your best, to Excellence, you will do what it takes to figure out your destination. You will know your source of inspiration. You will believe in yourself and know your own potential. You will always take personal responsibility with complete integrity. You will be consistently aware and make conscious choices rather than being in a subconscious, fear-based state. Gratitude will fill your soul and lead you to see and find the opportunity in every situation, in every challenge.

Excellence simply means being your best. It means learning from your mistakes. It means being conscious, remaining calm. Your focus, discipline, your grit are all components to lead you to excellence.

Achieving your goals so you can get to your ultimate destination and experience your own personal definition of success requires Excellence.

Having a positive ego is important. When your ego becomes overinflated, it is self-defeating in many ways. Huge egos emanate quite a negative energy and actually push people away. The goal is to attract leaders, mentors, and like-minded positive people to you, not to make them want to travel to another country. Puffed up, egotistical people only think they are being their best selves, but you and I know it is not reality. They are basically self-centered jerks.

True leaders have realized success because they give more than they receive. They are grounded, down to earth, and have balance in their lives. This is what applying the Principles of COURAGE so you can find the FIRE within you is all about. Being your best self will lead you to balance and to success.

So, how do you find balance in your life?

One of the best life balance exercises I've ever seen or done was during an eight-week group coaching program with two world-class success coaches, JT DeBolt and Renee Kamstra. The premise of the exercise is when your life has balance, you will be more productive, feel more fulfilled and be happier.

The exercise is called the Life Balance Wheel. Draw a circle on a piece of paper. Divide the circle into eight equal sections, just like cutting a piece of pie. Then write one of the eight categories of life as follows into each section of your circle: Physical, Financial, Business, Lifestyle, Mental Health, Spiritual, Family, and Relationships.

Next, you honestly rate yourself in each of the eight categories. The center of the circle is equal to zero. The outer line of the circle is equal to 10, which means you have complete balance in that category. For each section, draw a line in that section equivalent to your self-rating for the correlating life category.

When you are finished, you will have a circle within a circle, or rather you will have an uneven scattering of lines within the larger pie circle. Your ultimate goal is to take action so that each area of your life is rated so that you have a perfect circle within the greater circle. The closer your inner self-rating circle is to the circumference of the original circle, the more balance you have and the more fulfillment, peace, harmony, happiness, and success you will have in your life.

When your rating shows you are out of balance, it's time to do some work in the areas that are most out of sync. You will be much more effective if you work on one or two areas of your life. Attempting to work on everything all at once will just throw your life more out of whack.

Everyone in the group found this to be a very enlightening and self-empowering exercise. Make it a goal to complete this exercise within the next 24 hours, and you will know where you need to start focusing in your life to bring yourself more balance.

Excellence is what brings the 7 Principles of COURAGE together. As you strive to be your best self, learn these principles and apply them to your life. Start by writing your commitment on a piece of paper, then dating and signing it. That's right, make a contract with yourself. When you apply the 7 Principles of COURAGE and combine them with your focused commitment of doing the work, you will get from where you are today to where you want to be.

To prepare your COURAGE, you must understand and have:

1. Clarity of Destination
2. Origin of Inspiration
3. Unrealized Potential = Mind-set
4. Responsibility (integrity and accountability)
5. Awareness
7. Gratitude
8. Excellence!

Use the principles of COURAGE to forge the elements of fire. When you find the fire within you, your purpose and passion, and live your life with the elements of FIRE—Focus, Inspiration, Responsibility, and Excellence—you will be living life with passion, have more fulfillment, achieve your goals, and make progress toward your ultimate destination.

All of the principles are important. When combined, you will begin to realize the incredible potential lying within you.

Being your best self means doing (taking action), not trying. Take any form of the word "try" out of your vocabulary. There will be no more "should" thinking, only expectations of accomplishment. When you're stuck in "should" mode, nothing changes. Once again, *knowledge* combined with *action* is empowerment. Know this and live it. Commit to it.

An excellent action step is to write down the three most important actions each night you will take the next day. These actions must be ones that will directly lead to achieving your goals and get you closer to your destination.

Every day must be focused: know your intent, pay attention, believe in yourself, and know with certainty you will accomplish your goals. Be filled with gratitude for the incredible opportunity in every situation, past, present, and future. Reflect with a mind-set of gratitude on your past and empower yourself for the future. Remember, when you are filled with absolute gratitude, there is no room for fear. Gratitude changes everything.

With each challenge, you are growing, transforming, and building skill sets and your ability to achieve. To make sure you are developing a self-empowering mind-set, there are four questions from *Know How to Be Rich* by Dr. Robert Anthony you can ask yourself for each thought process:

1. Is it factually accurate?

2. Is it in your best interest?

3. Does it make your life easier or more challenging?

4. Does it get you what you want?

Conditioning yourself to follow this four-question doctrine will absolutely empower you. Remember that anything and everything that comes from a place of fear, such as stress, anger, frustration, hesitation, procrastination, trepidation, self-doubt, disbelief, worry, and so on, only exists in your mind. None of them are factual. It's all about your conscious choices.

There is no such thing as failure. When you are living each day with Excellence, you have the awareness to realize that the experience is in reality a building block, a stepping-stone to your success. From this point forward, believe in yourself. Visualize the excellent adventure of your life that lies ahead. Make your life the adventure you want it to be. Realize your potential and live your dreams.

There are two additional values which will form the cornerstone for your success...

CHAPTER THIRTEEN

CONSISTENCY AND PATIENCE: FOUNDATIONS FOR SUCCESS

Success comes from taking the initiative and following up...
persisting...eloquently expressing the depth of your love.
What simple action could you take today to produce a
new momentum toward success in your life?"
–Tony Robbins

Being consistent and having patience form the foundational cornerstone for achieving your goals and realizing the suc-

cess you dream about. They will help you as you apply the 7 Principles of COURAGE. You will experience fulfillment as you take consistent action to achieve your goals, and having patience will help you remain calm and focused as you begin to realize your full, innermost potential over time.

Success takes focus, discipline, vision, consistent work, and patience. Once you have your plan of action in place, these are the core characteristics on which you need to build and develop your self-empowering mind-set so you will make empowering choices to take action, get results, increase your self-belief, and tap into more of your potential.

Once you have broken down your action plan into the specific action steps you need to take, you must take personal responsibility for following through and taking consistent daily action.

It's important to understand that your worthwhile goals leading to your destination will not be achieved overnight. This is why patience is vital. Patience helps you maintain your mental composure while having clarity for your vision of success, and will help you focus on the process without being distracted by unreasonable expectations for results.

When you have honed your mind-set and combined this with empowering burning desire, a resolute commitment, consistency, and patience, you will be developing a true skill-set necessary for your success.

Often the most overlooked component for what it takes to be successful is the necessity to work on yourself. In order to achieve your goals and make your vision of success a reality, you must be the person, the leader that it will take to make this happen. It is extremely rewarding when others notice your transformation and most fulfilling when you see and feel the effects of your self-refinement.

Taking consistent *action* combined with patience will lead you to find a higher level of fulfillment and inspiration. As you begin to achieve your goals, your confidence will build, your skill-sets will improve, and your mind-set will develop an even deeper level of self-belief.

When your actions are not getting you closer to your goals, you must adjust what you need to do next. With the mind-set that there is no such thing as failure, you will be continually learning and improving your skill-sets by knowing what not to do in the future.

Spending a minimum of twenty to 30 minutes a day reading, listening, reaching out to mentors and individuals who have the success you dream of, and applying by journaling, planning, and doing the work, will lead you to amazing self-transformation and your life will begin to change. The energy you emanate will attract other inspired individuals and leaders to you. You will experience firsthand the empowerment of attracting incredible things into your life.

When you begin to reflect on how your life has transformed, you could be pleasantly surprised at how quickly everything changed. If you are impatient, nothing will happen quickly, if at all. Impatience is what leads many of the 96 percent to quit, often when they are getting close to achieving an important milestone goal.

Be consistent in focusing your attention on your *why*, your purpose and passion. Think it, believe it, and live it. Believe in yourself. Love yourself.

Every day, consistently strive to become a better person, leader, spouse, parent, friend, and to be better at what you do for your career. Figure out the source, the origin, of your inspiration and use it every day to fuel your desire, your commitment to follow through.

Take consistent, focused action to make these things happen and be patient. Know the more you learn, the more you are capable of, the more you are able to help others and the better the example you will be setting.

Be committed to taking action even when you don't feel like it. How badly do you want to achieve your goals and get to your destination? Taste it, feel it, crave it. The first step can be challenging, especially if you put it off. Invest 10 minutes right now and write down your goals to get things going and create the initial momentum you need.

CHAPTER FOURTEEN

WHAT WILL IT TAKE FOR YOU?

*Desire is the key to motivation, but it's determination and
commitment to an unrelenting pursuit of your goal—
a commitment to excellence—
that will enable you to attain the success you seek.*
– Mario Andretti

Are you where you want to be in your life? If not, how serious
are you about doing what it takes to change it? How committed are you to taking consistent action?

Have you reflected on why you aren't where you want to be? Have you found yourself blaming your situation on someone else, the economy, or on something you believe is outside of your control?

It's one thing to say you are serious and absolutely committed to changing your life. It's another thing to have the level of integrity to take personal responsibility and realize you are where you as a result of the consequences of your own actions or inactions.

Success is not going to be handed to you. Good fortune does arrive sometimes, but success is what you make of yourself and of your life.

Believe me, I know. I had it all and because of my own choices for the actions I took and inactions, things I did not do, I lost it all. I lost the complete financial freedom I once had. It took me a while to realize it was a direct consequence of my choices, and this was an amazing, eye-opening and soul-awakening epiphany.

After doing some in-depth reflection and self-work, I realized I could absolutely make it all back and more. With this revelation I began my journey of self-refinement. I started working on myself and will never stop doing so as long as I am breathing.

> *That some achieve great success, is proof to all*
> *that others can achieve it as well.*
> – Abraham Lincoln

You have incredible potential within you to become the person you must be to get to your ultimate destination. Reflect on this quote by Abraham Lincoln and open yourself to your potential.

Know that you can't simply read a book and transform yourself or change your life. You must consistently apply what you've learned. You must develop the leadership skill-sets it takes to realize your goals.

COURAGE to Find the FIRE Within is a practical guide to inspire you to do what it takes to invest in yourself to discover your passion, so you can live life in a passionately empowering manner. When you discover your passion, you will find inspiration and feel the energetic anticipation of each day to achieve your goals and get closer to your destination.

Do you get excited when you find yourself dreaming about what you want? How excited would you be if you knew you could get what you wanted? When you start forming your new mind-set of belief, visualize your destination as though you are already there. Use this anticipated excitement as rocket fuel to launch yourself on your incredible journey.

When man went to the moon, it started with a dream. Most people probably thought it was a pipe dream. The actual planning itself took a lot of time, and there was endless attention to technical and safety specifications and details. Not every action taken was correct. Specs had to be altered. Progress was slow and steady.

When Neil Armstrong blasted off with the rest of the crew aboard Apollo 11, it was the beginning of one of the most historic flights of all time. When Armstrong took that small leap from the ladder of the lunar landing module and his space boots touched the moon's surface, the accomplishment was summed up by his words that still echo throughout the universe:

That was one small step for man, one giant leap for mankind.
— Neil Armstrong

Commit to spending the time to learn and apply the 7 Principles of COURAGE. Then resolutely commit, meaning you will not accept any excuses, to apply them into your life. Do the work: whatever it takes to figure out your passions, set focused goals, take consistent action, and live each day with passion and purpose. Know what you want and be patient.

Find your inspiration and feel it in your soul; set an example for those you love, for everyone. You must know where you are in your life now and where you ultimately want to be. Know your destination and focus on the process, the actions you must take to arrive.

Understand that cause and effect applies to your actions. Every one of your actions (or inactions) will cause a specific effect. When you are not experiencing the effects in your life you really want, tweak your actions, or if necessary, completely change them with intended thought toward your destination.

Be aware of your choices as every one of them will get you closer to or farther away from your intended journey's end.

If you're sick of the pain from being where you are in your life, take personal responsibility to change the situation. If you know where you want to be, great. If not, that's okay too. You have to start at some point.

Dig deep to have *COURAGE to Find the FIRE Within*. Determine to resolutely commit to *Invest in Yourself to Discover*

Your Passion. Know you can transform yourself and become the person you really want to be so you can get to the place where you really want to be. Use the examples of others who have realized the world's amazing possibilities, figured out what they wanted, recognized their incredible potential, and taken consistent action…and arrived at their *ultimate destination* to spur yourself on. If they can do it, so can you.

For me, there is incredible inspiration from the fact that my brother had his dreams stolen by a heinous disease, yet in spite of the inability to speak or move on his own, he looked deep within himself and discovered a new passion and inspiration. Though he has been gone almost eight years, his efforts, his mission, and his inspiration will impact the lives of many for years to come. My brother had more excuses that could have held him back than anyone I know. Yet for him, there were no excuses.

So, what's your excuse? The reality is that your excuses are caused by your fears and are a figment of your imagination. You can't see, feel, smell, or hear them. The bottom line is, if you are truly serious and committed, there is no excuse. I challenge you to become one of the 4 percent of those who do what it takes without excuses.

This is my commitment to myself and to my family. Live up to your potential and absolutely and resolutely commit to impacting your own life and the lives of those you love.

Everything in the future is determined by what you do now!
— Unknown

Prepare yourself and you will definitely find the COURAGE to invest in yourself to discover your passion so you can live life passionately, the way you really want.

Take that first step and don't ever look back.

ACKNOWLEDGEMENTS

There are so many people to thank for so much throughout my life. For the specific purpose of *COURAGE to Find the FIRE Within*, I want to extend thanks to those who have inspired me, mentored me, taught me, supported me, or impacted me in any way that has contributed to and led me to write this book and to its being published.

I would like to begin with thanks to my younger brother and best friend, Chris Hobler. Though Chris lost his battle with Amyotrophic Lateral Sclerosis on February 16, 2005, his passion to make a difference for individuals with neurological diseases still impacts the world via Hope Happens for Neurological Disorders, the public charity my brother started to raise funds and awareness, and via The Hope Center For Neurological Disorders, one of the world's first collaborative research laboratories. Chris, I miss you and love you. Know you continue to inspire me every day.

My daughter, Alie, inspires me in so many ways. I know I have learned more from her than she will ever learn from me. Thank you, Alie, for not only being an incredible daughter, but for being an amazing young lady who is aware, sensitive, and really beginning to realize her own limitless potential. I love you un-conditionally and am so very proud of you, my sweet Alie Girl.

I never imagined the endless support I would receive in every area of my life when I first met Kathy Arnold. You are beautiful inside and out. Your intelligence, insight, caring for others and unconditional love set the bar for what loving relationships and friendship can be and mean. Thank you from the bottom of my heart. Know I love you more than I can ever tell you or show you. Thank you also for always supporting my writing efforts and for your unconditional willingness to edit my drafts! I con-sider you my best friend on top of everything else.

During the past few years, I have experienced the most dramat-ic transformation of my life. There has been a core group of in-dividuals who have consistently been there in various ways, in-cluding teaching, coaching, having insightful discussions, new empowering friendships, or setting an inspirational example for me and many others.

With this being said I would like to say thank you to the leader-ship of the PRO U community, particularly Jay Kubassek, Justin Woolf, Greg Davison and Matthew and Christine Kominiak. Louie Long, Dennis and Nikki Goff, Jane Selwyn-James. Know I value our friendship and our discussions. I extend my thanks to the entire PRO U community for your support and inspira-tion over the past two years.

Recently, I became a mentor for the Join Hands program, which provides mentorship for young teenagers in East St. Louis, Illinois. I would like to say thank you to Mike and Sheila Burton, who founded Join Hands. Mike, know I truly appreci-ate our discussions and our budding friendship.

I must say that without my third party support group, I would not have had the confidence in myself or the courage and commitment to bring this project to life. Thank you to the many of you, including Tony Robbins, Dr. Robert Anthony, Stuart Lichtman, Simon Sinek, Brian Parsley, Dale Carnegie, Thich Naht Hahn, Darren Hardy, David Bach, Malcolm Gladwell, Walt Hampton, and Ron Price. As it's impossible to mention everyone in this realm of transformational awareness, I would like to acknowledge everyone who is committed to doing what it takes to transform themselves and change their lives and who share their knowledge and inspiration. Know I am grateful for you and your efforts and that you inspire me.

I am grateful for my success coaching clients. Thank you for your support, your belief in me, for your commitment and hard work, and for challenging me to be my best. I have a feeling I have learned more from you than the other way around.

Thank you to Virginia Muzquiz for your endorsement and incredible networking and marketing training. You are an amazing woman and a true friend.

I would be completely remiss to not express my sincere thanks to the folks at Aloha Publishing. Maryanna Young, thank you for believing in me and helping me to further believe in myself. Your passion is contagious and your support amazing. Kim Foster, thank you for your insight and expertise in the realm of editing to solidify the content and bring it to life on these very pages. Thank you, Cari Campbell, for your incredible, insightful creation of the beautiful and inspiring cover design, and thank you to Shiloh Schroeder for your expedient and great work on the interior design. And thank you to everyone in a support capacity at Aloha.

Patrick Combs, the founder of MIGHT Club. Without my MIGHT Time, I would not have been nearly as effective or productive. Thank you for helping me to create my MIGHT and for setting a truly inspirational example to so many people. I look forward with excited anticipation to meeting you in person.

It's challenging to fully express my immense, heartfelt gratitude and thanks for the seemingly endless insights and ways in which my coach has helped me to help myself. JT DeBolt, you are an absolutely inspirational coach, empowering mentor, a lifetime valued friend, and just an amazing person. And many thanks to your wonderful heart-mate Mia, who does my SEO work, and is so insightful. JT, without you, I would not have had gratitude enter my life or had the courage to write this passionate work.

For the future, I would like to thank everyone from this point forward for how you impact my life, my writing, and further inspire me to pursue my passion of inspiring others to look within and to have the *COURAGE to Find the FIRE Within*, so they can live life the way they want, with passion.

To each and every one of the individuals above, I would like you to personally know that I am filled with profound and immense gratitude for who you are, what you stand for, for your integrity and for the impact you have had on me and for the contributions you have brought to this project. Writing this book has been a truly passionate, energizing, and transformational project wherein I have shared the culmination of my life's experiences, the lessons, the challenges, and the transformation. Without you, this literary effort would not be a reality.

Here is to you, to your success and to your inspiration to realize your goals and to eternally continuing to impact others so they can discover their passion and live their dreams.

ABOUT THE AUTHOR

PETER HOBLER
THE COURAGE COACH

Peter seemingly had it all. And he lost it all.

He had has several entrepreneurial business experiences including three ventures into network marketing.

In 1997, Peter built a dream house in Jackson Hole, Wyoming. In 2007 during the all-too-recent economic and real estate crash, he had to sell his dream home. He lost the financial assets he had come to take for granted.

He has always led an extremely active and exciting life. He played two varsity sports in college. He loves to ski, play tennis, travel the world, write, read, cook, spend time with family and friends. He has a true passion to inspire others to discover their passion and realize their potential.

Peter has an amazing daughter, Alie, with whom he loves spending time. Alie just may have more potential than anyone he knows.

The past 10 years have been a journey of seemingly endless eye-opening epiphanies, leading to self-awareness and the realization of the incredible potential waiting to be tapped and released into the world.

He has taken full personal responsibility for his life and has committed to pursue his passion of inspiring others by relating his life experiences, lessons and insights.

Peter has studied the stifling impact of subconscious fear. He has worked with professionals and mentors. He hired a world-class success coach to help him help himself.

The past two years in particular have led him on a journey of self-refinement and he has begun to tap into his innermost potential and has started to see his life begin to change in incredible ways.

He knows what his ultimate destination is: what he wants, where he wants to be, and who he wants to be.

He has a Plan of Action to get there.

Peter is the first to admit he is not yet where he wants to be and he realizes that as each goal is achieved, the self-transformation and his journey will be never ending as his goals and destination may change as well.

His passion, his purpose is to share with you, to help open your eyes to the potential within you, to inspire you to have the *COURAGE to Find the FIRE Within.*

Peter is down to earth, insightful, mind-set oriented and his relatability will draw you in, capture the essence of your dream-oriented potential and if you are committed, allow you to start on your own journey.

He is a previously published writer having 70+ published online articles on topics including Mind-set, Leadership, Communications, Achievement, Personal Growth, Success Coaching, Abundance and Prosperity, and Career Advice.

As a Success Coach, Peter inspires people to strive for excellence by being their best self for life, business and relationships. "I inspire people to wake up so they can begin to learn how to recognize and tap the incredible potential within them."

We all need a guide to provide insights and inspiration to spur us on to transform ourselves in order to change our lives, to be able to live life the way we truly want.

Let your journey to success begin here. Be determined to never let it end.

Open your eyes, heart and mind to the lessons, insights and epiphanies within these pages so you can discover how to have **COURAGE To Find The FIRE Within**, and *Invest In Yourself To Discover Your Passion.*